YOUR *Restoration* JOURNEY

Rediscovering your Faith & Yourself After Divorce

JEN GRICE

Copyediting and typesetting: Sally Hanan of Inksnatcher.com
Cover design: Jen Kline of LineOfHopeCreative.com

Ordering Information: Special discounts are available on quantity purchases by corporations, associations, and others. For details, contact the author at the email address above.

Your Restoration Journey: Rediscovering Your Faith and Yourself after Divorce/Jen Grice

ISBN: 978-0-578-84492-3
eBook: 978-0-578-84749-8

To all the women I've talked to and supported over the last six years since starting Surviving + Thriving Ministries. Without you, I wouldn't be doing what I do. It gives me great pleasure to live out my divine purpose serving divorcing and divorced women.

He has made everything beautiful and appropriate in its time. He has also planted eternity [a sense of divine purpose] in the human heart [a mysterious longing which nothing under the sun can satisfy, except God]—yet man cannot find out (comprehend, grasp) what God has done (His overall plan) from the beginning to the end.
—Ecclesiastes 3:11

Contents

Introduction

I started writing this book in early 2019 and completed it in December 2020. Obviously, we all know what happened in March of 2020—the United States was shut down and we were all told to stay home. This meant that some of the things I wrote in 2019 needed to be updated after COVID-19. It also shaped my life during that year, which started out really well but didn't end in the way I expected it to.

It also meant this book took much longer than I wanted it to. I felt the urge to complete it, but many times I just felt I could not write another word. It felt so fruitless, and I struggled to trust it was really what I should be spending my time doing. You will read about my struggles in this book. I share this authentically to show you that even seven years post divorce, life is not always perfect. We humans struggle. We can trust God and still feel anxiety over what is going on around us.

Toward the end of 2020, I knew I needed to complete this book. I knew so many women would benefit from these words, just as I did in writing them and reading through them before sending the manuscript off to my editor.

Over the last several years I've walked with and coached thousands of women through their divorce trial and through rebuilding their life after. I've seen women take many different paths. Some women lose their faith and fall back into the same types of relationships they were in before and during their marriage. They go out and search for another husband to repair and redeem their lives. This path may work out for some, but the majority of women who choose this route end up with more heartache, more that needs to be repaired, and no feeling of redemption.

I believe there is a better way. In my first book, *You Can Survive Divorce*, I explained what the world thinks moving on should look like.

"Most people associate 'moving on' to be returning to the dating world and finding their next spouse. Have you heard this before? 'When are you going to start moving on with your life?' is often said way before you are ready to start dating. The world has some sort of idea that the only way for a divorced woman to be happy is if she is dating and/or remarrying, like this is the only way God can redeem and restore her life. But I want to challenge that line of thinking and redefine the phase 'moving on' for Christians after divorce."

Before I even completed that book, I knew the what's-next question would land in my inbox, and it has many, many times. But I wasn't able to write this Bible study as soon as I'd published my first book because God had to take me through the restoration journey to see it for myself. I had to rebuild my own life and feel it was redeemed without dating or remarrying. I had to know it would work out if I did.

What am I supposed to be doing after I've come to accept my marriage is over and I need to move on with my life? This book is the answer to that question. I knew the few paragraphs in my first book would not be enough to sustain women through the years God has them working on healing, strengthening their faith, learning to love themselves again, and waiting to feel that everything had been redeemed. I also knew women would face more trials that would put their faith to the test. I, too, needed to know where to find that encouragement to keep going.

The feelings we experience during an unwanted divorce are like being on the Titanic while it's going under; the only difference is that we're sitting in a courtroom as they announce the word "divorced." I was the person running around the boat trying to save myself as it went under. Maybe you were too.

Now, seven years after my divorce, I still have not moved on, according to the world's standards, but I have learned how to sit still in the middle of a storm—even when I think I might drown. That's the point of growth and assurance in faith—to know that no matter what happens, when everything falls apart, you are held together by your faithful Father; to know that God is still redeeming everything and He will restore all that was taken.

This is not to say you can't date or remarry after divorce. I love being single and free to follow where God leads, but everyone's path is different. Someday I hope to find a partner I feel comfortable marrying, but I needed the years of my singleness to heal and rebuild and gain everything I want to share with you.

Many women do remarry and go on to live a thriving life. If that's you, you are welcome to read this book and gain the same healing from it. Parts of you may be healed, but there may be other parts that need work to grow into the relationship the Lord wants to have with you. In this book we will walk through how to repair your faith so it can grow stronger. Then you'll find your authentic self, the person God created you to be—His beloved daughter—so you can feel stronger as a woman and as a woman of faith.

As you probably already know, the journey may seem dark, but God's light and His Word will guide you, just as the Israelites were guided by His cloud by day and fire by night. There may be losses, but there is so much to gain. The biggest gains will be in your faith, as well as faith in yourself. Your faith will be the foundation on which you stand.

While earning my bachelor's degree at a Christian university, I learned an invaluable way to study the Bible, especially certain passages. This has helped me to learn and understand what God was trying to communicate to His people through the Bible, as well as how that applies to my own life.

"Exegesis" is the careful study of God's Word to discover the original and intended meaning of each passage. It can also include the historical and cultural backgrounds of the author, text, and original audience. Studying the Bible can be a difficult undertaking, but it doesn't have to be that way. Using this approach helps us to better understand what we're reading.

I have included exegetical commentaries after each assigned passage for you to read and write, but I suggest you do your own examination of the verses. Being an infallible human, I and any other author or Bible scholar could get the meaning wrong. You are free to gain your own understanding and apply that knowledge to your own life.

How to Use the Exegesis Approach to This Bible Study

The process of exegesis involves:

1. Observation: What does the passage say?

2. Interpretation: What does the passage mean?

3. Correlation: How does the passage relate to the rest of the Bible?

4. Application: How should this passage affect my life?

My Story

This shortened version of my story should help fill in the pieces missed throughout this book. I have three children, two girls and a boy. I worked outside of the home until a year before my youngest was born. After that, I was mostly a stay-at-home mom who was very active in my children's lives. I was the "room mom" whenever possible, helped coach softball, led Girl Scout meetings, drove kids to most of their activities, homeschooled the youngest two, and so much more. I also was slowly working on my associate degree and then my bachelor's, which I finally completed in 2016, after my divorce.

When I divorced in 2013, our oldest daughter, who was over eighteen years old, had already moved out of the home and was living on her own. At home still was my sixteen-year-old and my ten-year-old, both of whom were homeschooled at the time. Literally two years after that, my middle daughter moved out to live with her dad. As of writing this book, my youngest child is now seventeen years old and itching to leave as well, so I'm almost an empty nester. I've been through all of the stages one can go through as a parent, and as a single parent after divorce.

> If you're on social media and share this book as you're reading, or after you've completed the study, be sure to tag @MsJenGrice and #YourRestorationJourney so I can encourage you along the way.
>
> We're on this journey together. Let's get started!

Week 1
Where Is God?

SINCE, THEN, YOU HAVE BEEN RAISED
WITH CHRIST, SET YOUR HEARTS ON
THINGS ABOVE, WHERE CHRIST IS,
SEATED AT THE RIGHT HAND OF GOD.
—COLOSSIANS 3:1

The Presence of Faith

I was angry with God. I had been a Christian for well over a decade. I did all the right things. I was honest and full of integrity. I worked hard. I attended church services, participated in Bible studies, took the marriage classes, read many Christian books, worked for guest services, and mentored a needy child at the local elementary school. I was doing all these good deeds for my faith and expecting the rewards of an easy life and well-loved family. That was the promise—right?! I would be prosperous if I did what I was supposed to do.

On the outside, I looked like the "perfect" Christian wife and mother with all the right outfits, accessories, and makeup. I put in my time to look good on the outside and expected to get what I wanted. But on the inside, I was the prodigal's older brother. I was angry things weren't going my way. I didn't feel accepted or appreciated for all I had done or continued to do for those closest to me. I wanted my prayers to be answered. I wanted my marriage to be saved or for something bad to happen so my husband would see the need to repent and become a more righteous person, *like me*.

I prayed for him and over him—asking God to intervene and change his heart, remove his anger, end his adultery. I truly wanted my marriage saved, but I wanted a different husband even more. I wanted a man who loved me and who would honor his vows. I wanted a man of integrity. God didn't take my will for my husband nor for our marriage and make it His own. My house of cards and perfect-looking little life crumbled to the ground. I had to admit I was a failure at making everything perfect just by my actions alone, and that what I tried so hard to do didn't work. I couldn't save anyone. I had to ask God to rescue me from my abusive marriage. I felt I'd rather be alone.

Once my divorce was final, even in my anger, I could no longer live the lie. God didn't protect the outer package of the perfect family we'd created, so I needed to put up a wall to protect myself from further pain and hurt. In fact, He exposed my imperfections for all to see. I had put my faith in my own tenacity and in what I looked like rather than in the One I belonged to. My marriage, and all our material possessions, had become my idols of perfection. God had to take it all away to show me what real faith and living for Him looks like.

I both needed God and hated Him at the very same time. I felt Him close by but I wanted Him to go away and leave me like everyone else had. I was angry that this was the outcome rather than my plans for the future. As I share in my first book, *You Can Survive Divorce*, I told God I didn't want to be a Christian if it meant I would have to deal with all my heartache and struggle. I did not want to be divorced!

But through my healing journey, I learned I would need to experience my divorce in order to find my real foundation—my faith and my God, who was missing in my life. Women may lose their faith while going through a divorce. For me, I lost my faith during my marriage because I depended on the created, and myself, instead of the Creator. My world revolved around our family, our home, and how to make it all look better. The day my divorce was final was the first day of my slow walk back to trusting God for everything. I needed to be in His presence in order to heal. He was there but He still needed me to accept Him back in.

My Creator wanted to take me back to a relationship with Him. I was angry, expecting certain outcomes from my difficult divorce. I didn't want to lose everything, didn't want to start over in a new town to me, didn't want try to rebuild my life as a divorced woman. I didn't see how I was going to survive let alone thrive after all of this. I just wanted my old married life back! That wasn't going to happen. (And now, seven years later, it still hasn't happened. I no longer want that.)

I relate it to the Israelites leaving Egypt and Job losing his entire family at the very same time. Not only was I oppressed in my marriage, I was also worshipping my actions. I was trying to make my faith seen by others, thinking I could be an example, when underneath it all was my own flimsy infrastructure. God needed to take everything away to show me what I was really missing the entire time—Him!

God promises to care for His children while taking them through the wilderness (the Israelites) or after they lose every earthly possession (Job). He cared for me, even in my anger, while showing me I was cherished by Him—not the fake version I had built but my true authentic self, the person I was created to be.

Going Deeper

READ PSALM 16 AND 1 THESSALONIANS 3:7–12. DOES ANYTHING STAND OUT?

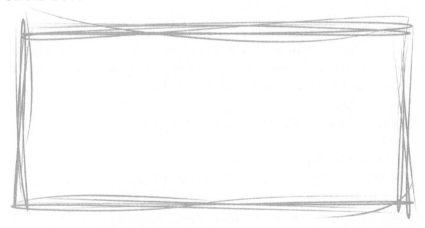

WRITE OUT PSALM 16:8 AND 11.

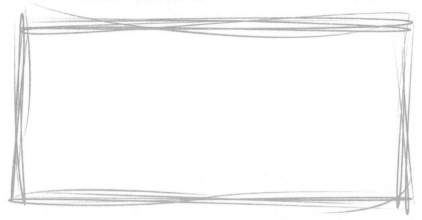

PRESENCE: "The state of being present; current existence; the immediate proximity of someone or something; an invisible spiritual being felt to be nearby; the impression that something is present."[1]

SYNONYMS

Being, existence, closeness, latent, omnipresence, proximity

AM I SEEKING GOD AND KEEPING HIM CLOSE?

IS MY ANGER KEEPING DISTANCE BETWEEN MYSELF AND HIS PRESENCE?

AS BAD THINGS HAPPEN, DO I BLAME GOD OR DO I SEEK HIM,
KNOWING HE WILL WALK WITH ME AND REDEEM EVERYTHING?

Biblically Speaking

When a building is constructed, builders need to start with a solid foundation to hold up the structure being built. Footings are used to distribute the weight of the building and secure it in place to the earth. Without a strong platform under a building, the brittle walls and floors will come apart and collapse. And when storms come, as they always do, any structure not secured to a rock-solid foundation can be easily destroyed.

The same connection could be made with a deeply rooted white oak or pine tree. Under the soil are roots that run so deep and are so connected to the soil that they hold the tree upright in the roughest of conditions. The wind will never stop blowing, yet these deep-rooted trees are not moved by the wind. They remain grounded in the soil below.

In philosophy, *hypostasis* is the underlying reality that holds everything up, just like a foundation.[2] A building's foundation or a tree's roots are often unseen because they are buried or concealed by what's above the surface. Just because you don't see it doesn't mean it's not there, but after any building is destroyed, or a tree is uprooted, you get to see what was under that surface. The same is true of the catastrophe of divorce. A foundation is exposed and you don't know which end is up. It can be a scary time to live in that destruction.

BLESSED ASSURANCE

Pain and despair have a way of changing a person's thinking. It can make you believe that because one thing is falling apart, everything will. Nothing will ever be different than what you're feeling right in this moment. If you're honest, you may feel alone when life comes crashing in around you. You can't see outside the entire forest because you're in the thick of the trees. There's a light at the end of the tunnel, but you don't think there is an end to the darkness.

But God sees! He gives you faith. He supplies you with blessed assurance.

> In the same way God, in His desire to show to the heirs of the promise the unchangeable nature of His purpose, intervened and guaranteed it with an oath, so that by two unchangeable things [His promise and His oath] in which it is impossible for God to lie, we who have fled [to Him] for refuge would have strong encouragement and indwelling strength to hold tightly to the hope set before us. (Hebrews 6:17–18 AMP)

Blessed assurance is an indication of a person's confidence in an unstable world. A person of faith doesn't depend on his or her own abilities, strength, intelligence, ingenuity, or any sort of magic. Assurance is trusting that God doesn't have the ability to lie, that He keeps His promises. Your faith is the glue that holds you together with Him when you feel like you're falling apart. You are so deeply rooted that when the wind blows, and you know it will, you will not be destroyed.

Faith is not a one-time act of saying "I will trust you" and then turning back to your old ways of thinking and acting. Faith is a daily, deep concentration on the good things to come, believing in His promises. It's knowing that underneath your human body, a solid Rock is supporting you. It's an acknowledgment that God is walking with you through any and all trials—even divorce. It's focusing on the promises you can't see but are confident in. It's when you keep trusting and believing instead of watching the wind as it blows and destroys everything around you. Faith is trusting God has something better in mind, even if you can't see where you'll end up just yet, because you're too focused on the destruction.

> I am the vine; you are the branches. If you remain in me and I in you, you will bear much fruit; apart from me you can do nothing. (John 15:5)

IN THE CLOUDS

When the Israelites were spending their forty years grumbling in the wilderness, struggling with their faith and idolatry, God sent them a constant reminder of His protective presence and guidance. Even in their lengthy struggle to give up their cultural traditions and gain the promised land, God didn't abandon them. Where did He hang out? In the clouds.

> By day the Lord went ahead of them in a pillar of cloud to guide them on their way and by night in a pillar of fire to give them light, so that they could travel by day or night. Neither the pillar of cloud by day nor the pillar of fire by night left its place in front of the people. (Exodus 13:21–22)

The overhead cloud of glory (or pillar of cloud) is also referred to as *ananei hakavod*—pronounced: ah-nah-A-hak-a-vard—a Hebrew phrase explaining how God was staying as close as a shelter over His children all day and all night. God was inside of each cloud and flame, preparing, guiding, and sustaining them.

You may feel as though God is far away or as if He doesn't care about the situation you're in. When you feel you can't be forgiven for the choices you've made, or you wonder if He even cares anymore about His children, look at the clouds. That's where providence (the protective care of God) is. He is near. You just have to look up!

No matter what lies ahead, God is faithful to be there and keep you grounded.

Anchored to the Designer of Faith

During my separation and the divorce process, my former husband refused to pay any of my bills—even with a status quo order requiring that he do so. My van had needed new brakes for some time, yet he was weaseling his way out of providing for, and even caring for, his own family. He had moved out, so if it didn't affect him and his immediate life, he didn't want to help. I was beyond frustrated about what to do. He had ownership of our joint finances and told me there wasn't any money in the account for these extras like groceries or new brakes for my van. I was left with zero dollars to feed my children or survive. This forced me to rely on God for everything and to trust in His promises and provision of our daily bread.

Having money in my checking and savings accounts had always been my security. It's not about showing others I have money (because I don't tell anyone what I have) rather than wanting to know that if an emergency arises, I can cover that expense. Not having an emergency fund is still scary for me because I know the storms of life will happen; there has never been a time they haven't. I hate the feeling of uncertainty or wondering how we'll survive. My security was put to the test the entire year it took for my divorce to be finalized, and even in the years since. After the divorce, I was forced to start my life over with only a few years of monetary support—no retirement, no savings, no completed college education, and absolutely no job experience. Although I'm grateful for the spousal and child support he's paid for a few short years, it didn't make up for the years I'd spent building, supporting, and contributing toward our debt-free future and retirement. I'd clipped thousands of coupons and shopped for deals so we could drive nice vehicles, have the occasional vacation, and save. I can't get back anything that was lost, but I *can* move on with faith that God holds my future, and even my finances, in His hands. The biblical character Job lost everything and was then given back twice that was lost. I don't even need that; I just need the security of knowing I won't be homeless or unable to meet my basic needs.

I could very easily focus on my lack of retirement funds, lack of a financially secure career, and lack of all the other things that were physically and financially lost because of infidelity and divorce. I can choose to believe God's promises and stay connected to Him or I can get angry by dwelling on what I don't have, what I believe I deserve, and how long recompense is taking. The devil prefers we do that, but God calls us to walk in faith, and I'm sure He prefers me to do that instead of going it alone to get everything I desire. Instead, I focus on the things I cannot see—the promises He shares throughout His Word—and remain thankful for His provision of daily bread, which is all I really need.

I was released from a toxic relationship, where image mattered, to walk in God's purpose, where God gives me my image. He guided the Israelites to leave what they had always known—the security of the pharaoh to provide for them—to follow God into an unknown future and His purpose for them. In the process, they found God's grace—after grumbling and staring at the storm for more than forty years—and the only true King. That's my story too. I try not to grumble so I will see His promises as well. But I'm authentic, a quality I know God can and does handle well. This is the reason I'm writing this book too—not because I'm perfect and have everything figured out, but actually quite the opposite. God said to start writing this book before I felt my faith was solid enough to even talk about faith after divorce. But through writing, editing, sharing with others, and releasing any shame (that scary stuff you don't want to share with other humans) that might come from these pages, I grew my roots deeper into God's foundation. This is His story, and He wanted me to tell it. I'm merely a vessel who one day will be gone. My hope is that this book helps one woman to grow in her faith and feel secure about her future.

Now, seven years post divorce, I'm more securely rooted. These roots won't let anyone or anything blow me over. The storms of life might be scary and the wind will blow, but I am anchored to God, the designer of my faith. I can make my plans but God will direct my path. He is walking with me into the promised land.

Going Deeper

READ MATTHEW 8:23–27, MARK 4:35–41, AND LUKE 8:22–25. DOES ANYTHING STAND OUT?

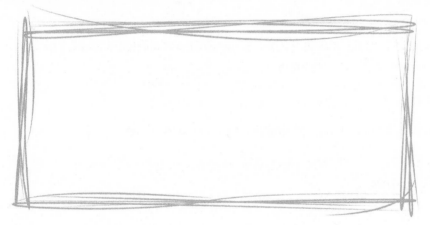

WRITE JEREMIAH 29:11.

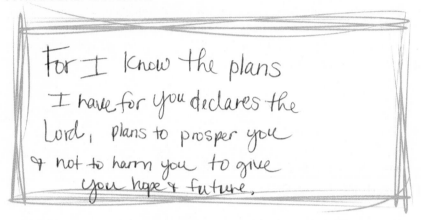

For I know the plans I have for you declares the Lord, plans to prosper you & not to harm you to give you hope & future.

PLANS: "To think carefully about a series of actions that you need to take in order to achieve something."[3]

SYNONYMS

Arrange, blueprint, design, engineer, organize, work out

AM I FOCUSED ON THE STORMS IN FRONT OF ME OR THE FUTURE GOD HAS PLANNED?

Storms in front of me

CAN I TRUST GOD'S PROMISES AND PLANS, EVEN IF PART OF HIS PLAN INCLUDES MY DIVORCE?

Yes!

WHAT IF THOSE PLANS ARE FOR SINGLENESS?

Biblically Speaking

The verse you wrote out today is often interpreted incorrectly. People often believe it to mean you should apply it like a quick fix to your immediate struggles. Or they think that if they ask God to stop the storm, He will do so immediately, just as Jesus did after his nap in the boat on the lake (Matthew 8:23–27). But when you look at the verses around Jeremiah 29:11, you see a very different picture. Jeremiah 29 is a letter to the captive Jews still in Babylon. Jeremiah told the people they would return after seventy years—*yes, seventy!* (v. 10). This wasn't going to be a swift return. Jeremiah was suggesting they learn to thrive in the midst of their exile. God had a plan, but even though the struggle would continue, God had not, nor would He ever, forsake them (v. 11).

In order for God to achieve something, He needs to have a plan. His timing of those plans is often not the same timing as you may have. God has had a plan from the beginning, and His perfect plan includes His perfect timing. Sometimes that's seventy years later. The Jews were going to have to spend many more years experiencing this situation. Many would never see the promised end, but God was with them. He is the hope everyone needs in the midst of life's storms.

> He doesn't stop the storm or take away the problem or heal the illness, but He walks with you through it. Those are times when we must trust Him. Again, if He has said to you, 'Let's go to the other side of the lake,' He will get you to the other side of the lake! It may not be through placid waters, but you will arrive:

> God is our refuge and strength, A very present help in trouble.
> Therefore we will not fear, Even though the earth be removed, And
> though the mountains be carried into the midst of the sea; Though
> its waters roar and be troubled, Though the mountains shake with
> its swelling. (Psalm 46:1–3) Really, David? You won't even be
> afraid if the earth is removed? You won't be traumatized if great
> mountains start crashing into the sea? David had learned to trust
> his God no matter what. (Greg Laurie, *Hope: For Troubled Hearts,*
> *Those Who Lost Loved Ones, Single People, Those Who Grieve,*
> *Those Facing Crisis, Prodigal Children, Failing Marriages*)

Just like the disciples in the boat, you may find it easier to focus on the
storm rather than trust you won't be harmed. Jesus was fast asleep so the
disciples thought things were outside of His control. But when Jesus asked,
"Where is your faith?" He was saying: Why would I let this storm harm
you, silly people?! Faith is not about keeping all eyes on your
circumstances and being worried about what's going to happen next
because when you stare too long at the storm, you can put it at the center
of your life. If it's your main focus, you start to believe it will ruin you; but
when you keep your eyes on Jesus and the promises God has made to you,
you know this storm might bruise you, you may even be changed, but you
will not be destroyed.

> A broken reed He will not break [off]; And a dimly burning wick He
> will not extinguish [He will not harm those who are weak and
> suffering]; He will faithfully bring forth justice. (Isaiah 42:3 AMP)

Since you know He only has good plans for you, you can trust that
whatever storm you're experiencing in your life has a purpose. That storm
would have never done any harm to those men unless God had accounted
for it from the beginning. Instead, the purpose of the storm was to show
them that Jesus, with God's power, is always more powerful than our
circumstances, even when they look really bad. He was able to sleep
knowing in the end things would be fine again; this was just a storm. No
need to worry about it!

And even if Jesus and the disciples had died that day, where were they
going? If you know where you're going after death, who holds your

salvation? What do you have to fear? Not even death can harm you. Your soul is safe anchored in Him.

STAY ANCHORED

In order to stay upright and hooked to a solid foundation, a ship that is being blown around in a storm needs an anchor—a heavy object created to tether a vessel to the seabed. An anchor could also be a person who provides stability and connectedness in tough times. Humans often need an anchor during storms to keep them upright and stable. In the Bible, the word "anchor" is used symbolically to represent faith in God. The boat in which Jesus was fast asleep was connected to Jesus the anchor. He knew God was bigger than any storm and that His power would guide them through the storm and oversee what happened to the boat. Jesus was able to calm the storm.

Even when God doesn't calm the storm, He's still with us, holding us close, leading us through. Staying connected to God does the same for women of faith. It provides hope and unshakable confidence that God is who He says He is. He's still on the throne, and His will is the only way to live a life of peace, even during the biggest trials and the strongest storms.

> This hope [this confident assurance] we have as an anchor of the soul [it cannot slip and it cannot break down under whatever pressure bears upon it]—a safe and steadfast hope that enters within the veil [of the heavenly temple, that most Holy Place in which the very presence of God dwells]. (Hebrews 6:19 AMP)

Faith in the Healer

I have been plagued with chronic pain, illness, and weird aliments on and off for my entire life. I remember always having some sort of stomach issue as a child. This usually involved milk or eggs, both of which I still try to stay away from. As a teenager, I started having migraines that caused nausea and vomiting. I was also hospitalized for an allergic reaction to a sulfa drug and when my digestive system stopped working, for no apparent reason. While married, I still struggled with some of these same issues, especially the migraines and stomach issues. After two of my children were diagnosed with a milk allergy, and the other with lactose intolerance, I stopped drinking cow's milk completely. I'd also get upper respiratory infections that would cause a gagging, painful cough and eventually pleurisy. I dealt with a lot of pain that baffled doctors and specialists for many years. After forty years on this earth, my doctors and I finally figured out I internalize all the stress in my life, which causes me to be physically sick. I probably had repeat stomach ulcers my entire life without ever knowing or getting them treated. I also had repeat sinus infections. Finally, in December 2012, the same month of my divorce separation, I was decisively diagnosed with systemic lupus erythematosus (lupus, for short). All the systems and issues I had dealt with my entire life now made sense. It was all tied to this.

I've been told stress is the main cause of my internal pain and external symptoms, so now part of my healing is staying as stress free as possible.

After my divorce, I learned I needed to find better ways to handle the stress and triggers in my life. I've had to kick out anything or anyone who causes me a lot of unnecessary stress. I've learned to take time for self-care and have limits in order to keep myself healthy. I've learned to have a stronger faith that everything will work out without my assistance instead of getting really stressed and feeling pressured to take care of everyone else but myself.

Because of verses like Galatians 2:20, I can only assume these would be the same things Jesus would tell me if He still walked the earth today. Jesus responded to the human need for love, acceptance, and healing. He sought people's faith in God's healing power to make them well. Although my lupus might not be cured by miraculous healing anytime soon, I can be heart healed. I can find ways to live anchored to God and stay deeply rooted in my faith. Finding healing after divorce is not always easy. I liken it to the bleeding woman (in Mark 5). We can see many types of doctors, specialists, coaches, and healers, but only Jesus can cure our emotional bleeding and our need for a foundation of faith.

Going Deeper

READ HEBREWS 11 AND MARK 5:21–43. DOES ANYTHING STAND OUT?

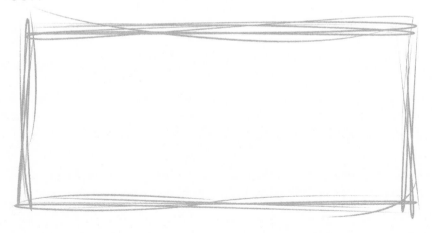

WRITE LUKE 1:45.

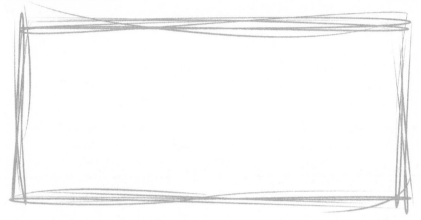

FAITH: "Is, in general, the persuasion of the mind that a certain statement is true. Its primary idea is trust."[4]

SYNONYMS

Admission, certainty, confidence, dependence, expectation, reliance

WHAT HOLDS ME BACK FROM HAVING CONFIDENCE AND HOPE IN GOD'S HEALING POWER?

Biblically Speaking

The bleeding woman (in Mark 5) understood what you may be feeling and going through right now. She had been ceremonially unclean and impure for twelve years (see Leviticus 15:25). Blood inside the body meant life but blood poured out meant death (see Leviticus 17).[5]

This woman was an "untouchable," a second-class citizen to those who lived the Jewish law and said she was unclean. But not to Jesus! Anyone else would have been unclean for even touching her. But Jesus knew exactly what she needed. It was her faith that brought her out of the crowd seeking Him. How daring she had to be to take those steps, to speak those words, and have faith that just touching Him would bring her healing. She knew the greatness of God and had the boldness of speech to match.

She knew suffering (Mark 5:26). She fell to His feet (v. 33.) She was moved to action by her faith. Jesus stopped to acknowledge her and her faith. "Jesus turned and saw her. 'Take heart, daughter,' he said, 'your faith has healed you.' And the woman was healed at that moment" (Matthew 9:22). She was blessed because she had faith that He was who He said He was. *Makarios* is Greek for "blessed." It describes a believer receiving God's favor in return for his or her faith, that is, God's grace and mercy for His children. God has shown us this by giving us a Messiah.

There are no drive-through answers to divorce and the healing we all need after it. There is no immediate healing or quick fix pill. Healing takes time. If only we all could just touch a piece of His clothing and be healed straightaway. But while I believe in miracles, healing usually doesn't happen so quickly after longsuffering. We have to allow Him to do the necessary work in us in order for us to fully heal.

It's a creature comfort to know that the One who created you also knows how to heal you, both inside and out. It took months or years for your marriage to end and to create this divorce season; it will take months and years to heal from the rejection and the pain. You may not have the answers to why for many more years to come after that, but you will still heal, knowing God has you in His mighty hands. In your hurt and broken heart, reach out to Him and have faith He will heal you. You have to give all the broken pieces of your shattered heart to Jesus. He is a gentle doctor. He'll bandage your wounds and protect you from future harm.

"He heals the brokenhearted and binds up their wounds" (Psalm 147:3). God wants you to learn more about Him and His healing so you can have a changed heart and mind. Healing does that to you; it grows your faith and strengthens your belief system. His love shows you He can be trusted—He keeps His promises. God's children become witnesses of these fulfillments just as the disciples did when walking with Jesus. They lived a life of faith because they walked with the Healer.

Faith and Christianity are about a relationship, not a religion. Christians are Jesus followers and worshippers, not a bunch of people who can follow a list of rules from the Bible. Jesus came to set you free, and you are set free and receive His favor when you choose to know Jesus and put your faith in Him. Faith also underlies or motivates the visible action of doing as God has asked you to do, not because of His rules but because you know He wants you to do what is best.

Many of our biblical heroes were able to courageously trust in the unseen substance of faith while outwardly obeying God (Hebrews 11). They trusted in their true foundation.

- Noah built a boat, trusting God had a reason for asking him to build it (Genesis 6, 8).
- Abraham left his homeland to gain his inheritance and then he was willing to sacrifice his son. He had made a covenant with God and trusted His long-term plan (Genesis 17, 18, 19).
- Job and Ruth lost everything, yet they still trusted everything would be redeemed (book of Job, book of Ruth).
- Sarah and Mary believed they would bear a child in an unusual way, knowing God was faithful (Genesis 17, Matthew 1).

God may not fix a broken marriage, but He promises to heal you and make you whole. That's His restoration story. He is the writer and you are the main character. Your story is still unfolding, and you are in His book. It's your job to keep moving forward into healing and start the next chapter of your life.

Complete in Faith

I think somewhere in my growing-up years, I started to believe getting married and having a husband was what would make me whole. It would make me a godly woman and getting married and having children was my purpose. What else was I here for? I don't blame anyone, especially not princess movies, because I've never related to those anyway. But somewhere I picked up this message: you are only complete when you are married and have children. It was the box I put myself in. It was just the way things were supposed to be.

Now, as a divorced woman, I see this is a couples' world, especially at many churches—they tailor their programs and sermons for families consisting of a husband, wife, and little kids. This can make us divorced women feel that without a husband, we're not really welcome in that church, or that we're not a family because we're incomplete. I hear this often from divorced women. They, too, don't know where they belong without a husband and/or young children.

Since my divorce, not only have I felt a lack of a church home but also of an earthly home. I don't have family in town, and there aren't many of my family members still alive to even have a town. Because we moved so close to the end of my marriage, I haven't established roots anywhere. I don't have a permanent home. Shortly after my divorce, I assumed I would need to find another husband to make me feel at home and complete. But as I grew in my learning and my faith, I've learned that was a fleshly feeling and an earthly belief, and not something required for heaven (actually, every single human, married or not, goes to heaven alone). God reminded me that with Him, I'm always family. Even though I only have one child still left in my home (my other two are grown and have their own families), we are a family too. And when I'm an empty nester, I'm still in His family.

My earthly body yearns for warm breezes, white sand, and beautiful blue waters. But even if I succeed at my goal of moving to a warmer climate, this earth is not my home either. My soul will always feel homesick and weary for the promise of life after death because neither the earth nor anyone in it can fill that void but Jesus.

Going Deeper

READ JOHN 3:22–36 AND COLOSSIANS 2:6–15. DOES ANYTHING STAND OUT?

Write Out John 3:29.

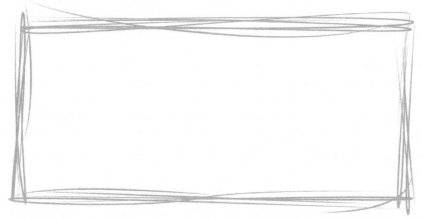

COMPLETE: "To make (something) whole or perfect; to finish making or doing (something); to bring (something) to an end or to a finished state."[6]

Synonyms

Entire, faultless, fullness, not-lacking, perfect, thorough

Do I feel incomplete without a husband?

.

In what ways do I still feel tarnished by the fact that I am getting a divorce or am now divorced?

Biblically Speaking

Most divorced women—both Christian and non-Christian—believe remarrying after divorce will complete them. This feeling is very normal, and even though most experience that feeling, it's not the truth. This is one reason the divorce rates for second and third marriages are so high. People are trying to fill the emptiness in their hearts with another person instead of looking for completeness through Christ, which is a necessary step before dating again.

> Was our father Abraham not [shown to be] justified by works [of obedience which expressed his faith] when he offered Isaac his son on the altar [as a sacrifice to God]? You see that [his] faith was working together with his works, and as a result of the works, his faith was completed [reaching its maturity when he expressed his faith through obedience]. (James 2:21–22 AMP)

The Greek word *pleroma* describes the act of being filled or completed by your Creator, God. It is both being made perfect and being perfect in your Creator's eyes. The same divine power to complete you was transferred to Christ, the only sinless Person to walk this earth. He sees His children as perfect because He's already died with all your sins once and for all, and you've gladly received that forgiveness. "For God was pleased to have all his fullness dwell in him, and through him to reconcile to himself all things, whether things on earth or things in heaven, by making peace through his blood, shed on the cross" (Colossians 1:19–20). You can say you believe in a God who created the universe, the Father of Jesus—the Savior of the world, but faith is so much more. You have to know that through His death on the cross, you are given a unique opportunity to be reconciled to Him and His glory. His death was not just for other people but for you as well.

Paul asked in prayer that we would be given complete knowledge of His will and spiritual wisdom (v. 9). This wisdom comes from the Holy Spirit, who lives in you when you are united with the Savior, Jesus Christ. He is the source of your Christian life and faith. There is nothing you need to bring with you or obtain in order to be given completeness. You don't have to try to add anything to that finished work. Jesus's death on the cross made you pure and blameless. Christ embodies all the fullness of God, and in Him you find your fulfillment. Your faith in that fact, and the wisdom you gain from going through your storms with His presence within, just like He did, makes you whole and complete. The process of trusting, enduring, and building your faith is being worked out day by day as you walk with Him, little by little. Your job is just to receive and accept this precious gift of forgiveness.

> It is a great thing to learn faith: that is, simple dependence upon God. It will comfort you much to be assured that the Lord is teaching you dependence upon Himself, and it is very remarkable that faith is necessary in everything. 'The just shall live by faith,' not only in your circumstances but in everything. I believe the Lord allows many things to happen on purpose to make us feel our need of Him. The more you find Him in your sorrows or wants, the more you will be attached to Him and drawn away from this place where the sorrows are, to Him in the place where He is. (J. B. Stoney)

Even in the process, you may face more struggles and more trials. God doesn't promise a life free from storms; you know they will come. Whether you are newly divorced or many years out, you feel pain and grief for what was lost. You may still struggle emotionally, physically, or financially. You are still waiting for the promise of restoration and redemption.

King David also wondered how long he would have to suffer until healing or completion came, saying, "My soul is in deep anguish. How long, Lord, how long? Turn, Lord, and deliver me; save me because of your unfailing love. The Lord has heard my cry for mercy; the Lord accepts my prayer" (Psalm 6:3–4, 9). You may groan and feel incomplete because your earthly body has limitations. It's never perfect. Impatience is of your very nature as you wait for your earthly story to be complete. You're a new person in Christ but you still yearn for the new body you will be given after life. God was not ignoring David's prayers and He's not ignoring yours. God is not some jerk who doesn't care or just wants to punish sinners (all of us). God loves just as Jesus loved! He has mercy on you. He wants you to accept His grace. He realizes your fears and He understands your need for answered prayers. You'll see everything has worked out for good, and you'll feel complete only in Him, just like He promises.

Only God can make you whole—not things, not people, and not even worldly love. And a restored life doesn't always include being remarried. Instead, God's desire is for you to grow closer to Him, trust Him, and experience the contentment only He can provide. You are being loved into wholeness. You only need to be patient and endure.

> Once you were alienated from God and were enemies in your minds because of your evil behavior. But now he has reconciled you by Christ's physical body through death to present you holy in his sight, without blemish and free from accusation—if you continue in your faith, established and firm, and do not move from the hope held out in the gospel. (Colossians 1:21–23).

Alive in Faith

If you've ever attended a charismatic church, you know the excitement and enthusiasm that can go on during a church service. People are falling on the floor, speaking in tongues, and dancing around the room with exuberance. They are filled with the Holy Spirit, who is alive and moving on their behalf. There is an energy in the joyfulness and worship.

I haven't always attended this type of church. Since deciding to be a Christian, I've attended many different denominations. I've mostly attended churches where everyone just stands semi-motionless as we sing a few worship songs, bow our heads to pray quietly, and then sit quietly as the pastor shares a few stories and a Bible verse. I don't have a preference as I'm fine with most service types, but I enjoy being moved by the Spirit and really getting into the worship music. (Yes, I'm the one with my hands in the air, waving them around like I just don't care.)

When I was going through my divorce, we attended the Assembly of God church that held a weekly DivorceCare support group. A couple of us divorcing ladies would sit together next to the group leader and her husband. On one of the Sundays, my young son and I went up to the altar to be prayed over. I was feeling very stressed and in need of reassurance as I prepared for the battle in court. The legal process was getting to me. My lawyer, his lawyer, and my soon-to-be-ex had created a settlement agreement that wasn't pleasing to me; it would be very hard for us to survive from the day the divorce was finalized; plus, everything that was promised to me was excluded from that offer. I felt as though I was being ganged up against, three against one. No one was listening to what I needed, and they really didn't seem like they cared. On that Sunday morning, I asked to be baptized in the Holy Spirit. Just then I felt like I was born again, and although I had never believed someone could be so moved by the Holy Spirit, I fell to the floor. Either overcome with emotion or being moved by the power, I'm not sure, but there I was, surprised to be there. After a few minutes on the floor, I got up a changed person. I was now full of faith and peace. I felt confident God would take care of me and my two children still living at home.

In my exhaustion from trying to get through the legal process of divorce, I wasn't interested in "finding my faith" or even going to look for it. But thankfully, I learned it was a free gift I didn't have to work for. I just needed to be open, willing, and able to fully accept the Holy Spirit as the power over my life. That was the day I fully surrendered, accepted God's gift, and was willing to give up everything, even my marriage, to follow Him. It was the day I knew there was hope and I had faith everything was going to be okay, even without a husband to take care of me. After that service, I stood up for myself and said what I needed before signing any further papers. I knew I was being taken for a ride legally, so I said, "Stop!" I wasn't signing something I couldn't agree to, and I was willing to go in front of the court judge, knowing I had God as the ultimate judge on my side. Then they started listening. My divorce was finalized just a couple months later, on December third, and I walked away with new confidence and the gift of perfected faith.

Side note: Because my ex-husband wanted to be divorced as quickly as possible, he agreed to create the court order I was willing to sign. We ended up agreeing just before the deadline given to go to trial, which would have dragged things out much longer. This is not the norm for most cases, and things could have gone really bad for me in front of the judge if he had not agreed to my divorce terms. I always suggest you do what is best for you when deciding to stand up against this tough opposition.

Going Deeper

READ EPHESIANS 1. DOES ANYTHING STAND OUT?

WRITE EPHESIANS 1:18–20.

ENLIGHTENED: "To give intellectual or spiritual light to; instruct; impart knowledge to."[7]

SYNONYMS

Advise, counsel, educate, guide, instruct, reveal

HAVE MY EYES BEEN OPENED TO THE WISDOM AND COUNSEL OF THE HOLY SPIRIT?

IN WHAT WAYS, IF ANY, AM I HINDERING MYSELF FROM ACCEPTING THIS GIFT?

Biblically Speaking

In Ephesians 1, Paul was writing to the Christians of Ephesus about God's great plan to bring Christian unity. He wanted the Ephesians to have a greater understanding, and a grasp of their glorious destiny and divine power of persuasion that was within them. Paul was shining a light upon the truth within their hearts, if they only would accept it.

The Hebrew word for faith is *pistis* (pronounced pist-us), which means "persuasion, moral conviction; especially reliance upon Christ for salvation."[8] Divine persuasion is a moral conviction for truth. Believers receive it. It's an experience of hope even when you feel you've hit rock bottom and have nothing left. It is then you look to Jesus. It's the place you are in when you hear Him say, "You've trusted Me with your life after death (your salvation). When will you trust Me with your life here on earth?"

Isaiah prophesied that Jesus would bring hope to the world. Before Jesus ascended up into heaven, He promised His disciples He would send the Advocate who would never leave them, the Holy Spirit (John 14:16–17). The Spirit not only brings power and comfort but also wisdom. Paul was asking them to open the eyes of their hearts so the Spirit could enlighten them to the truth and the reality of true faith. Spiritual enlightenment helps you do things in your life. It gives you full comprehension of entire situations, even if you don't see all of the details or what is going on behind the scenes. It helps you to know important truths. God opens your eyes to these truths as you walk through trials. When you seek Him, you can feel His presence through the Holy Spirit. You understand that no matter what happens or where you go, God is always with you in the journey.

> He delivered us and saved us and called us with a holy calling [a calling that leads to a consecrated life—a life set apart—a life of purpose], not because of our works [or because of any personal merit—we could do nothing to earn this], but because of His own purpose and grace [His amazing, undeserved favor] which was granted to us in Christ Jesus before the world began [eternal ages ago]. (2 Timothy 1:9 AMP)

Jesus is the hope of all the world. "This fulfilled the prophecy of Isaiah concerning him: 'Look at my Servant, whom I have chosen. And his name will be the hope of all the world.'" (Matthew 12:17, 21). Before Jesus's death, most people would talk to God through someone else. Humans still lived under the law of Moses, making sacrifices in tabernacles, the earthly dwelling place of God's presence. When Jesus died, God moved out of this earthly dwelling and became accessible to all.

Enlightenment helps you to understand what God has already done and provided: salvation and eternity. This is only your temporary home, but it's where you live out God's plans for you. It's where your purpose comes alive. God doesn't want you living on earth without assistance from heaven. The Holy Spirit was given to you as a gift on the day you first believed. This Companion has been with you since that day. From today's reading, you learned that when you believed in Christ, He identified you as His own by giving you the Holy Spirit (v. 13). Jesus left you this gift so you'd never be without Him walking beside you, guiding you, and imparting you with wisdom from above. This Holy Spirit is God's presence with you, just like Jesus with His disciples, to work out your growth and faith.

Faith is not something you have to work really hard to obtain. You don't have to study your Bible more to be full of faith. There is nothing you can do to earn it. It was given to you as a free gift. You only need to accept it and grow in it. Allow it to be alive in your spirit. Where does your hope and faith come from? The Holy Spirit is your internal GPS, guiding you to healing and wholeness each and every day, all the days of your life. And after your spiritual eyes are opened to see the hope that is before you, your physical eyes will be opened to see the wonders God has for you each and every day, such as a beautiful sunset, a new bloom on a spring day, and the miracle of a child's birth.

Week 2
Bread of Life

JESUS DECLARED, "I AM THE BREAD OF LIFE. WHOEVER COMES TO ME WILL NEVER GO HUNGRY, AND WHOEVER BELIEVES IN ME WILL NEVER BE THIRSTY."
—JOHN 6:35

Motive for Pain

Almost eighteen years ago I gave birth to my third child without any pain medication. I can still remember the horrendous pain. At that point there was nothing anyone could do about it—too late for drugs. No one wants to experience pain, but we often do so to gain something wonderful in the process. Thankfully, there is joy when bringing a new life into this world and becoming a parent. Without it we probably wouldn't do it more than once, or at least, I wouldn't! (The pain of losing a child or delivering one to heaven is much worse. I can't even image that pain. My heart hurts for you if you've lost a child.)

The painful mourning and grieving process after divorce and loss is not an easy one. At least childbirth is over in a few hours (or days). In our divorce, we can't immediately see any good outcome from this pain; there is no baby. As I shared in my first book, I was emotionally hemorrhaging every place I went, especially at church. I just wanted someone to make it stop. But no one could. It was too late for any treatment or procedure to fix it. No one could put my marriage and family back together the way it was before all of the affairs. I had done everything I could and everything that was advised. My conscience was clear. It was now time to accept my divorce. I had to walk through the sewage of it, allow Jesus to heal the pain, and accept this was my new life.

While I was dealing with my pain and the destruction, a family friend had her basement flooded with water, as well as some of the drain field. Everything that was in a cardboard box was ruined. Many of the items were mementos of her children's childhood, including pictures. Although I had never experienced that myself, I could have empathy for the loss and the cleanup afterwards. This is exactly what I was doing in my own life— cleaning up a huge mess I was not prepared for, and I was feeling the losses. All my friend could do was have faith and hold onto hope that one day the mess would be cleaned up. She still had her memories and her children, and new memories could be created. It was a struggle, but she got through it. I eventually got through my destruction as well and have gone on to have a thriving life. You will get through your destruction cleanup and mourning process too, holding on to your hope and faith. Hope believes something good can come out of the bad. Faith is the assurance that everything will work out positively, even when we feel like all hope is lost. It reminds us we've survived everything so far in life, and with God, we'll survive this destruction and mess too.

Through my divorce and healing journey, I've gained a new life. I found the person I was created to be and He's reshaping me to be more like Him. I'm not exactly the person I was before my marriage. I've gained so much wisdom and joy, and I am finding the confident woman I was before my heart was destroyed by betrayal and abuse. My new life includes my relationship with God and the enlightenment of the Holy Spirit. I know He walked with me through this valley and has brought me to where I am today. As we walked together, I learned I could trust Him during any trial. He would walk with me through the mess and create a message. As my trust grew so did my faith.

Pain is an identifier, meaning something is wrong that needs to be removed or fixed. When we feel the pain, we want to find out the reason and get it fixed. We often go to see a doctor who gives us something to lessen the pain and suggests ways to cure the problem, or at least minimize the symptoms.

God, the Creator of this world, is the only One who can fix our heartache and brokenness. When we come to Him with all the pieces of our shattered heart, He promises to be gentle as He carefully and kindly puts it all back together—most times restoring the broken pieces to better condition than before.

> God will allow evil only to the degree that it brings about the very opposite of what it intends. (Timothy Keller, *Walking with God through Pain and Suffering*)

Going Deeper

READ ROMANS 8:18–30, 1 CORINTHIANS 15:19–23, AND PSALM 25. DOES ANYTHING STAND OUT?

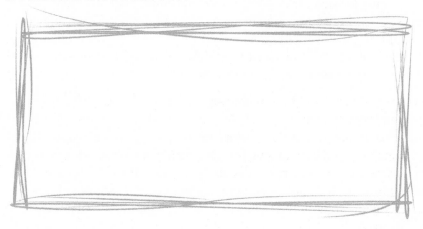

WRITE OUT ROMANS 8:28.

FOR GOOD: "For one's benefit, even though it may not be enjoyable or desired."[9]

SYNONYMS

Beneficial, fruitful, helpful, profitable, suitable, useful

HOW AM I HEALING THE PAIN AND WORKING THROUGH THE DESTRUCTION?

HAVE I ASKED GOD TO WALK WITH ME?

WHAT HAS BEEN A BENEFIT OF MY NEW LIFE AFTER DIVORCE?

Author's note: Writing down the good that has come out of painful experiences helps us to keep things in perspective. Also, writing down what was lost helps us to mourn and grieve.

Biblically Speaking

Living in a broken world equals pain and suffering. Everyone has to experience it at some point in life; no one is immune. But it can be very hard to see any benefit coming from your own painful experiences, especially while you're experiencing it. Hurting people often ask: Where is God when I am hurting? Why do I have to continue to struggle? What's the point of all of this pain? When will it end?

Romans 8:22–23 compares the pain of childbirth to that of the pain we feel here on earth. Your body wrestles with your redemption that is to come and what you're experiencing on earth. No one has arrived at his or her final destination, so you ache for the day when His promises are fulfilled. You are a child of God, but Paul said your adoption is not complete until you come to the end of your life. In times of trouble, the hope is that one day you will meet your Creator and Father face-to-face, and all pain and destruction will be fully healed and the gold hidden in it revealed. Until then you are living through the birth pains as you patiently wait for that day. This hope should be at the forefront of your minds so you're not distracted by the devastation around you.

Romans 8:28 affirms your hope that all things, not just some things, will be worked out in a way God sees as perfect. God is sovereign, which means He has everything accounted for and worked into your purpose—His long-term plan for your life. It may not be how *you* envisioned your life to look but it will be how *He* sees things best worked out.

Walking with God through this pain will see you through. His motivation is lovingkindness. He wants to use your triumph to bring Him glory. He wants to use your pain and suffering, and how He's worked it out for good, to show the world He is still on the throne.

> Not to us, O Lord, not to us; But to Your name give glory; Because of Your lovingkindness, because of Your truth and faithfulness. Why should the nations say, 'Where, now, is their God?' But our God is in heaven; He does whatever He pleases. (Psalm 115:1–3 AMP)

JOB KNEW PAIN

Job wanted to know the reason for his suffering. His endurance and moral character were put to the test when God allowed the devil to send destruction to his home and family. Job's story shows that even a righteous man can struggle with resentment and disapproval of the lack of God's intervention when times are tough.

> God wants us to choose to love him freely, even when that choice involves pain because we are committed to him, not to our own good feelings and rewards. He wants us to cleave to him, as Job did, even when we have every reason to deny him hotly. That, I believe, is the central message of Job. Satan had taunted God with the accusation that humans are not truly free. Was Job being faithful simply because God had allowed him a prosperous life? Job's fiery trials proved the answer beyond doubt. Job clung to God's justice when he was the best example in history of God's apparent injustice. He did not seek the Giver because of his gifts; when all gifts were removed he still sought the Giver. (Philip Yancey, *Where Is God When It Hurts?*)

In the middle chapters of the book of Job, lamenting Job laid his anger upon God. God and Job argued back and forth. Job didn't pretend his pain didn't exist; he just strongly handed it back to Him, showing his pain and hurt. Through his pain and the loss of all of his possessions, Job turned to

God for answers and comfort. God could handle this pain. He can handle all human emotions.

In the end, Job's story is a reminder that God is sovereign over all, even over the devil's tricks. He uses the bad things to show you the strength of your faith and perseverance through it all. In the end all will be worked out. Jesus won the war on the cross, so even though Satan still has power, he doesn't have the ultimate power. God allows Satan's destruction because He knows if you stay connected to Him, you'll make it through. Without your earthly troubles, what would be your need for Him, your faith, or His lovingkindness? This pain and suffering are not how it's supposed to be, so it hurts—often both physically and emotionally. But when you feel pain, it connects you to the source of your healing. You gain intimacy with God (Job 42:5) and learn to trust in His restoration of everything. All of the healing might not take place here, in the present time, but you will be redeemed with glory in eternity.

JESUS (GOD IN THE FLESH) KNEW PAIN

Jesus needed to feel pain so He could know what humans feel when they are suffering and in pain. He walked this earth to fully understand what humans experience. Not only did He battle with the temptations and torture of the Satan and his forces; Jesus was also treated with cruelty by other humans. Then He died a painful death after being dishonored and betrayed by those closest to Him. Jesus felt the very same pain you have, so He understands. Jesus cried out for God to take this burden from Him, just as we humans do, yet He knew God's will would be done. You need to hold onto that same thought. Your will be done, Lord!

> God allows what he hates to accomplish what he loves. (Joni Eareckson Tada, *The God I Love*)

In the most painful moments, when your heart is broken and you don't know how to fix it, is when you invite Jesus in for comfort and healing. You invite Him in to heal you, to walk with you in this wilderness season, to keep you from giving in to the devil's tricks, and then to provide everything you ever need. As you learn and grow, being refreshed by this living spring, you are given access to God and His long-term plan for healing your pain and for empowering your life.

Author and speaker Priscilla Shirer suggests you pitch a tent and live in your pain just for a little bit, just as the Israelites did. In order to get through it, you have to feel it, experience it, and get a little comfortable in it.

> Even when we've begun to get a handle on some of the reasons why He might allow the wilderness, we still want to know how we can make it through. I know when I'm in the wilderness of uncertainty, with all those piercing 'why' and 'how' questions hanging over my head, the last thing I want to do is pitch my tent and just camp out for a while.
>
> I don't want to settle in and get comfortable with this part of the journey. (Priscilla Shirer, *One in a Million: Journey to Your Promised Land*)

DAVID TAUGHT US HOW TO LAMENT

In Psalm 25, David lamented about his life, the pain he felt, and the pain he had caused God. This was the season he was in. Twice he stated he put his hope in the Lord. David knew God is the author and creator of faith, even while he continued to struggle. The world is not our home yet humans try to find hope here. Hope can only be found in Him and the future He planned for you, long before you were even born. Only God can bring perfect comfort. His hope is a strong and trustworthy anchor for your soul (week 1, day 2.) Just like David, you face suffering. Not because you've sinned, although all have sinned and fallen short of God's expectations, but because through your struggles your faith is being made stronger. You're learning endurance. Each day you're learning to trust in Him more and more. God wants to reshape you into His image. As you read last week (in Hebrews 12), you need to keep your focus on the Lord. He has created and will sustain your faith. It can't be lost or taken away. He will watch over your faith, care for it, and pray for you as needed. You can groan in your pain, especially while on this wilderness journey to restoration.

What's God's plan for pain? The devil brings it but God will not waste it. He can use it to help you learn to loosely hold onto everything and everyone else while continuing to holding tightly onto Him. Pain causes you to need Jesus and His healing. The pain chips away at your character, but receiving His healing during your pain makes your soul more complete in love so you become more like Jesus.

Even though you didn't plan for this destruction, God will use it for good. Romans 8:28 is a promise. The storm is not good but all of God's outcomes will be. One of those outcomes may be a stronger relationship with your Creator or with your brothers and sisters in Christ, but God's goal is always to pull you back to Him, to walk with you, to help you realize He is all you ever need now and forever.

Appeal for Prayer

Joseph's story is one of my favorite stories of the Bible. If you've read my blog or any of my other books, you've probably heard me say that before. I can deeply associate with how he struggled with dysfunctional family issues and with his problem with befriending people who just wanted to use him and then blame him. Much like Joseph, I've felt marginalized much of my life. My family of origin, as well as my married family, belittled and silenced me. I felt forced to suppress my voice, intuition, and any gifts given to me by the Holy Spirit. But God has worked through all of that pain and used it for good "to save many lives" (Genesis 50:20).

I didn't have a father in my life while I was growing up. I think my father wanted to be there but it just didn't happen. During the '70s, when I was a child, most mothers were automatically given physical custody and allowed to make all decisions. I don't ever recall my father having any visitation rights. This allowed my mother to move us from living in the same city as my dad to living several states away, where he wouldn't have access to me. I never got to decide for myself if he was a good dad or not. I know my mother did the best she could with what she knew at the time. She gave me many values, including a strong work ethic and determination to get things done, which has helped me to succeed in life. But she also took away the value of family and loyal relationships. She moved us around a lot, so I don't have a set home to go back to. And after she and my father both passed away, before my divorce, I was left with no immediate or extended family to have relationships with. I have many long-term friends, but having no family left a void in my life.

When I accepted Jesus as my Savior in 1998, my Christian mentors told me I gained a new family. I was now adopted into God's family, with many siblings. I also learned God would be the Father I never had and so desperately desired. That felt amazing to me. I talked to God whenever and wherever I wanted. I would wake up in the morning and talk to God while I showered, while I did my hair, and while I commuted back and forth to work. When I was angry, I told God. When someone cut me off in traffic, I asked God to help keep me from having road rage—something I had struggled with. I asked Him for safe travels when weather or darkness threatened the drive, especially when I feared hitting a deer.

Praying became the way I would ask for what I needed. I felt His presence with me always. At first I had rather selfish requests. I just wanted my needs met. Sometimes my talking to God was like sitting on Santa's lap, where I would tell Him what I wanted to make my everyday life better. But as my relationship with Him matured and I started to understand His character, I was able to seek Him more deeply. I believe those initial prayers of a Christian, early in our walk with Jesus, are answered so we know God is really there and wants to give us the desires of our heart. We need that constant affirmation that He is for us and will never leave. I know I needed that during the early years. As we mature, we start to understand that unanswered prayers are not a sign of God denying us. He hasn't gone anywhere, and He is helping to strengthen our faith and endurance for the road ahead.

When I went through my divorce, after many affairs and a couple of reconciliations, I knew God wasn't going to answer my prayers the way I wanted Him to. After all those years, God didn't change my husband, as I'd requested. He didn't create a more peaceful home and marriage. That was on my husband, and he used his free will for other things. He allowed my husband to have affairs that damaged our marriage beyond repair.

If I had an earthly dad, I'm sure I would have called him daily to lament and seek his wisdom about what I needed to do next in my life. I can envision the relationship I would want to have with him—one of care, compassion, and lovingkindness—but since I don't have a father or mother to reach out to, I reach out to my heavenly Father instead. He is always available, ready, and willing to listen. My prayers became more about getting me through whatever I faced. Talking to God is comforting and therapeutic. He is my middle-of-the-night therapist. After twenty-two years of being a Christian, I know deep down that even if He is not currently giving me the life I envisioned, He is still here for me. Our relationship is deeply rooted in faith, and I can trust Him, even if this divorce and subsequent hardship wasn't my will. Instead of communicating just my needs, I now also communicate my frustration and worry. During my divorce and healing after, I lamented often in prayer. I knew He could accept all my anger and hurt feelings because He had felt all those deep feelings at some point as well.

He knows what we're experiencing and everything we've been through. God weeps with us as we cry out for Him. He may already know what we're going through but explaining it to Him gets it all out. And He exchanges our hurt feelings for His peace and the knowledge that everything will be worked out and someday come to an end.

Going Deeper

READ MATTHEW 11:25–30 AND 1 THESSALONIANS 5:16–18. DOES ANYTHING STAND OUT?

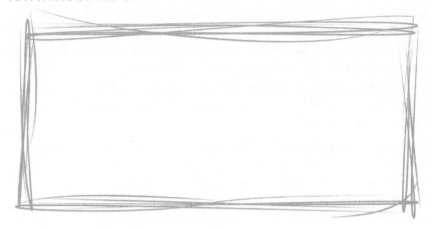

WRITE OUT 1 THESSALONIANS 5:17.

CONSTANTLY (OR WITHOUT CEASING): "all the time or often"[10]

SYNONYMS

Continually, continuously, frequently, regularly, persistent, steadily

AM I FILLING MY LIFE WITH PRAYER TO THE HEALER OF PAIN?

WHAT COMFORT CAN BE FOUND FROM HAVING A CONSISTENT PRAYER LIFE?

HOW CAN I TURN MY FOCUS FROM SEEKING HUMAN COMFORT TO SEEKING GOD'S COMFORT?

Biblically Speaking

Jesus prayed. His life was filled with prayer. Jesus praised His Father and acknowledged His great wisdom through prayer. Jesus prayed when He was baptized. He prayed before He picked His twelve disciples and before He walked on water. He taught His disciples how to pray through the Lord's Prayer. He cried out for God to take the burden of death on the cross from Him. Jesus knew it was the Father's will but He prayed it anyway. He knew God was with Him because He and the Father are one (John 10:30).

Jesus prayed because He wanted to stay connected to the Father He loved and communicate with Him. He knew He needed to focus on His oneness with His Father. He prayed God would protect His disciples from the Evil One. He prayed with expectation that God's plans were best and that without God, He could do nothing better.

HOW OFTEN SHOULD YOU PRAY?

Two people cannot have a relationship without ever speaking to one another. Prayer is done anytime you're talking to God. Paul encouraged believers to pray constantly, but that doesn't mean you need to be on your knees every waking second. Thanks to Jesus you have instant access to Him 24-7-365. As you're talking with the Lord, you're establishing and growing the relationship. The point of praying continuously is to stay connected to the One who gives you your confident hope and provides for your every need. It becomes easier to keep going, to step forward in your faith while worrying less when you are connected to the Creator of all living things, your heavenly Father. You stay deeply connected to God by speaking to Him, hearing from Him, and feeling His presence. You put your hope and confidence in Him.

The Hebrew word *shema* means "to hear or listen with respect for the speaker." Even more, it means "to pay attention to what the Lord is saying to you, how He's saying it, and why He's saying it." And it includes your response—how you listen to what He's saying and doing what He's asking of you. Humans are often very poor listeners, even with two ears and only one mouth. God asks you to have ears to listen to what He has to say. You can't hear Him if you don't speak to Him, seek His wisdom, and then listen. He could be saying the very thing you need to hear, when you need to hear it.

HOW DO WE PRAY?

Jesus talked about how to pray (Matthew 6).

1. First, we honor the Father for being the Creator of the earth.
2. Then we repent, ask, and yield (pause to listen/hear).
3. Lastly, we praise God for all He has done.

Amen! (claiming the truth).

> This, then, is how you should pray: 'Our Father in heaven, hallowed be your name, your kingdom come, your will be done, on earth as it is in heaven. Give us today our daily bread. And forgive us our debts, as we also have forgiven our debtors. And lead us not into temptation, but deliver us from the evil one." (Matthew 6:9–13)

King David was an avid "pray-er." He lamented [expressed deep grief or sorrow] when he needed assistance and protection from his enemies. He cried out in desperation and pleaded for God's mercy. David demonstrated humility, personal helplessness, sincerity, and faith in God's power to do what no one else could.

The disciples sincerely cried out to Jesus in the boat, scared for their lives. They didn't worry about waking Him. They just knew He would be the only One to save them in that helpless moment.

> Job's grief was expressed with powerful emotion and soaring rhetoric. He did not 'make nice' with God, praying politely. He was brutally honest about his feelings. And while God did—as we will see later—forcefully call Job to acknowledge his unfathomable wisdom and majesty, nevertheless, God ultimately vindicated him. A Bruised Reed He Will Not Break It is not right, therefore, for us to simply say to a person in grief and sorrow that they need to pull themselves together. We should be gentler and patient with them. And that means we should also be gentle and patient with ourselves. We should not assume that if we are trusting in God we won't weep, or feel anger, or feel hopeless. (Timothy Keller, *Walking with God through Pain and Suffering*)

David and Job had the heart to seek God and had faith in His power and His promises. They knew how to pray to God, four hundred-plus years before the birth of Christ, and they knew why it was important to pray in all seasons, for all reasons. There is really no wrong time or wrong way to pray.

> Is anyone among you in trouble? Let them pray. Is anyone happy? Let them sing songs of praise. Is anyone among you sick? Let them call the elders of the church to pray over them and anoint them with oil in the name of the Lord. And the prayer offered in faith will make the sick person well; the Lord will raise them up. If they have sinned, they will be forgiven. Therefore confess your sins to each other and pray for each other so that you may be healed. The prayer of a righteous person is powerful and effective. (James 5:13–16)

Invitation to Worship

After deciding to follow Jesus, I loved going to church and singing along to the worship music. I'm thankful to have been living in the Bible Belt of my state, where there were a few radio stations broadcasting Christian or worship music 24-7. Surprisingly, I even found a couple of Christian music CDs at my local music store. This was in 1998, before Christian music was mainstream and before iTunes, so it was nice to have options for listening to worship music between church services. I felt the heart call to worship and to turn my attention toward God. The music kept me reminded of His promises and encouraged me; they still do. As I worshipped and praised Him, I felt His presence and His loving grace upon me. It became, and probably still is, my way of saying, "I'm open to your presence, God. I'm here and ready to surrender it all to You." His invitation and my response bring us together. Singing a song has become not only my praise but also my communication with Him.

It's easy to forget to worship, easy for me to get back into an old routine of not listening to praise or worship music, especially if I don't get into my vehicle—where I have all the Christian stations on preset. Even as I write this, with daytime talk shows running in the background, I am reminded that I can switch my TV over to Pandora radio and put on one of my favorite Christian stations. Right away my heart is calmed and I'm open to hear what God is saying to me through His music and His Word. Sing and worship with me about heaven to a song like "I Can Only Imagine" by Mercy Me, or about how Christ is my all in all with "In Christ Alone" by Stuart Townend & Keith Getty, or about how good God is with "Good, Good Father" by Chris Tomlin.

When I started dating my husband, after knowing him for many years, he came to church with me and proclaimed himself to be Christian. Within a year we were married at my hometown church, in a spiritually moving and lovely wedding. I even moved away from my Christian family to live closer to him and his family. I quickly learned there weren't any Christian stations in that part of the state, just a whole lot of country music. The loss of my support system of Christian mentors and community caused a decay of my faith. As the years went on, the affairs kept happening. I found that worship was the only thing that was keeping me standing. I felt that invitation to come back to God and only worship Him. It became obvious that I could be easily pulled away from putting God first in my life and worshipping Him. At some point, Christian music became much easier to find on the radio, and I was able to purchase songs for my iPod.

During our multiple marital separations, I even started fasting for the first time in my life. At the time I saw fasting as a way to turn God's ears toward my prayers for reconciliation and restoration. He was going to bring my husband back home and he would never commit adultery again, thanks to my faithfulness in Him, my prayers, and my fasting. I was overjoyed when after a short few months, he did come back, saying he was repentant and wanting to be the husband God wanted him to be. But that initial dedication became an empty promise. After the third affair, I was totally committed to listening to only Christian music and worshipping God, no matter what kept happening. I think that is why I had such an easier time when the fourth and final affair happened. I knew God was calling me back to put Him at the center of my life and not my marriage or a husband. As I shared last week, God had to remove my husband so I would keep God at the center, where He belonged. I worshipped my marriage and the title of wife more than I did Him. He was jealous for me, and I needed a reminder that I needed God most of all. Also, I needed to learn that prayers and worship were to grow a stronger faith in myself, not just get what I wanted in this life.

During my divorce and after, I stopped questioning God about why this was happening to me and started praising God for rescuing me from this horrible cycle of adultery, abuse, and idolatry. He wanted to give me a better future—a future filled with peace and security in Him and a life of purpose rather than the chaotic life I had become used to. Now, I've rebuilt my life on His solid-rock foundation instead of on shifting sands that can easily be pushed over by worldly things and music. Now, I know that no matter who leaves my life and no matter what troubles come my way, He will always be there. I just need to remember to keep Him at the center and not try to put anyone else in that place. It's through worship and worship music that I'm able to stay encouraged and deeply rooted.

Going Deeper

READ JOB 1, PSALM 100, AND PSALM 138. DOES ANYTHING STAND OUT?

WRITE JOB 1:21.

PRAISE: "To express one's respect and gratitude towards (a deity), especially in song."[11]

SYNONYMS

Adore, applaud, boast, cheer, exult, glory

AM I STILL ABLE TO WORSHIP AND GIVE PRAISE TO MY CREATOR, EVEN THOUGH HE ALLOWED THIS DESTRUCTION INTO MY LIFE AND FAMILY BECAUSE HE CHOSE TO GIVE US FREE WILL?

IN WHAT WAYS CAN I BE REMINDED TO WORSHIP THE CREATOR AND NOT THE CREATED?

Biblically Speaking

In your pain, hurt, and destruction, you have two choices. You can turn away from God, saying you refuse to worship Him—He who allowed this separation or divorce to happen. You can allow your divorce to make you think God is not for you but only against you. Many women say they will never trust another man again, including God. You could question His sovereignty, thinking He's not controlling anything and permitting your spouse or ex-spouse to get away with all these things. You can be so angry that you don't seek Him for comfort or healing, which allows bitterness to take hold in your heart. How many people do you know who've married their anger and bitterness and now expel it in every relationship and experience? How sad, because even when humans mess up, lie to God or others, don't flee from sin, and get in trouble, God doesn't hold on to any anger. He's perfect and forgiving and forgetting when His children repent. He's always there waiting for you to come back to Him, no matter how far you've gotten off course.

Alternatively, instead of turning away from God and all things that worship Him, you can choose to suffer well. Take time to work on your healing. Pitch your tent there while knowing life has its seasons of pain, hardship, and then new growth. We will all face some sort of calamity or catastrophe while feeling uncertain about the future. You can choose to give thanks for the glory that is ahead, after the storm is over. Hold on to the hope that He will work things out for good. Choose to worship without conditions, without limiting God of His purpose and plan for turning this pain into something good.

Job was called a blameless man, even though he had a lot of possessions and then lost everything, even after arguing with God and showing his anger about all the losses. His friends blamed him for the destruction he was facing, yet after losing everything, Job immediately worshipped. How could he worship when he felt such grief?

> Worship will get you through the toughest times of your life because it shifts your focus from the problem to the Problem Solver! (Unknown)

Job did so because he knew the Creator's plans were greater than his own. He knew that even if he never got his possessions back, God is always who He says He is. He knew all the loss in the world didn't compare to what God has to offer—grace and salvation. In his grief, he tore his clothes, shaved his head, and fell to the ground to worship (Job 1:20). Then he did something many have a hard time with: he did not blame God (v. 22). Worshipping doesn't deny your pain or diminish your suffering; actually, it allows you to acknowledge it before God—not because He doesn't see or know but because revealing your pain draws you closer to Him. Sin doesn't cause bad things to happen. Sin came into the world long before you were even born. Job was an honorable man, but his only issue was that he questioned God as to why this was happening. In response, God said: "You as a human are not God and won't always know the reasons behind why bad things happen." Job endured his loss without knowing why and without becoming angry and bitter.

In the end, the Lord returned everything to Job, blessing him with double of what he'd had before. God's restoration story is that He will return all that was lost, even though everything belongs to Him. Humans arrive on earth with nothing, so everything we have is what He has given us—His abundant blessings, the best being a relationship with Him. Hopefully we will all leave this earth with a relationship with the Creator.

GIVE THANKS THROUGH WORSHIP

Psalm 138 is a song of praise and worship, of giving thanks. (Be sure to read and digest it fully.) David stopped to give wholehearted praise, goodness, and glory to God. He encouraged himself in hope, knowing that because he lived in a fallen world, troubles would come his way, but that in the end God would work out His plans for each human's life. Worship is not just going to church on Sunday morning, singing a few songs, and listening to a sermon. It also means incorporating it in each day. Putting God at the center means He's part of our morning, noon, and middle of the night. In the dark you can still worship, be encouraged, and find your hope in Him. John Piper says "the key to praising Christ is prizing Him." He wants you to live all of your life as a worshipper.

FAST AS A FORM OF WORSHIP

If you can safely fast without hurting yourself or your health, fasting helps to keep your eyes on Christ. Fasting is a sign of worship, especially when you're hungry for His will and presence. There are huge misconceptions around fasting. Many people believe you should only fast when you're asking God to answer a prayer (what I believed too). You may have heard about churches or other groups fasting to bring healing to someone with cancer or some other terminal illness, but that is not exactly the main purpose for fasting. Instead, fasting is a way to cultivate your hunger for God and grasp a deeper connection with Him.

Jesus said, "When you fast, do not look somber as the hypocrites do, for they disfigure their faces to show others they are fasting. Truly I tell you, they have received their reward in full. But when you fast, put oil on your head and wash your face, so that it will not be obvious to others that you are fasting, but only to your Father, who is unseen; and your Father, who sees what is done in secret, will reward you" (Matthew 6:16–18). Your reward is not always an answered prayer, but by denying your craving for earthly nourishment, you'll be filled with heavenly sustenance.

> Therefore bread was created for the glory of Christ. Hunger and thirst were created for the glory of Christ. And fasting was created for the glory of Christ. Which means that bread magnifies Christ in two ways: by being eaten with gratitude for his goodness, and by being forfeited out of hunger for God himself. When we eat, we taste the emblem of our heavenly food—the Bread of Life.

And when we fast we say, 'I love the reality above the emblem.' In the heart of the saint, both eating and fasting are worship. Both magnify Christ. (John Piper, *A Hunger for God*)

Appetite for Soul Food

As I've been writing this book, I have been deep into the Bible and growing in my understanding of the Scriptures. I'm reading all types of commentaries and Bible dictionaries and listening to sermons on these different topics so I can present the best information possible to guide you through this time.

I sat up in bed this morning after a nice two-hour discussion yesterday with my Christian mentor, knowing I needed to take a few minutes to just sit and talk with God. This has now become my morning routine. I have an alarm set to Pray! every morning. Sheila has been my spiritual and life mentor since I became a Christian more than twenty years ago. God speaks to me through her many times. And I do the same for her on occasion. In our conversation, I wondered, *Am I really feeding myself the nourishment that my soul needs?* as we discussed soul food. I think I'd been craving for more than what I'd been feeding on. I was reminded that my frustration about my circumstances was because I was undernourished, and I knew I could do worship more and worry less about my uncertain future.

I love all Christian music. I get excited about reading nonfiction self-help books like my first book *You Can Survive Divorce*, and I enjoy listening to great preachers explain what they saw in the stories of the Bible. But they don't compare to just sitting with Jesus, hearing what He wants me to know, or reading the Word of God for myself. That takes work, like preparing a large meal that tastes so good while you're eating it. Sometimes it just seems easier to warm up a frozen meal or go to a drive-through for a quick meal. It's less hassle. Less work. That's what I mainly prepare these days as I embrace the empty nest that is right around the corner in my life. If I'm going to create a big meal, it's because I can easily divide it up into many small containers for quick meals for the week, or because my teenage son is actually home for dinner.

When going through my divorce, just opening my Bible made me cry. I sobbed and sobbed on the pages as I tried to digest what I was reading. Eventually, I could no longer see through my own tears to read anything on the page. So I just prayed and wrote in my journal.

> *Lord, I believe in you and I seek your healing.*
> *I want to get through this, but I just don't know how.*
> *Until I can stop crying, can I just lay at your feet?*

That's where I stayed for a long time until each day brought fewer tears and more hope. I nourished myself with music, books, and preaching until I was able to open the Word of God and hear what He had to say about my future.

As I shared previously, I was fasting during my separations, and not always by choice. Often I just couldn't eat anything because of the tremendous stress. That tends to be, albeit a poor one, my coping mechanism. Instead of eating for comfort, I don't eat. Although I'm not hungry, I do keep myself hydrated. (I learned that lesson after passing out a few times after not eating.) I have a responsibility to take care of myself and keep myself nourished. My body needs nutrition until I am able to eat again. The spirit is the same way, craving nourishment to stay encouraged and to keep moving forward in faith. I can survive for a short time on quick-fix meals, but eventually I need to consume the nutrients my soul needs to continue to thrive in this life. Without God's presence, His worship, and His comfort, I can do nothing.

Many have an appetite for soul food but are only feeding on it just enough to survive, exactly like I had been. God would prefer we have a soul that is thriving. It often becomes easier to feed ourselves last, whether that is physical food or spiritual food. This is not healthy. Not only will we find our bodies weak, but our faith becomes weak as well.

Going Deeper

READ JOHN 6:22–59, LUKE 7:44–50. DOES ANYTHING STAND OUT?

WRITE JEREMIAH 15:16.

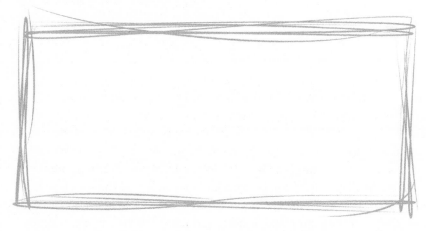

DEVOUR (OR ATE): "To read quickly and eagerly; be totally absorbed by a powerful feeling."[12]

SYNONYMS

Absorb, consume, enjoy, feed on, ingest, relish

AM I CONSUMED BY THE WORD OF GOD OR BY MY CIRCUMSTANCES?

HOW CAN I ABSORB MORE OF WHAT THE LORD HAS FOR ME AND STAY NOURISHED?

Biblically Speaking

You were created to crave. Without knowing it, you could be hungry—hungry deep in your soul where your faith and security live—hungry for hope, the hope only God can provide. Negative people feed on their circumstances, looking for worse to happen, and it does. Positive people feed on the hope that things will work out. Faith is the confident hope your soul craves. "Faith comes from hearing the message, and the message is heard through the word about Christ" (Romans 10:17). When you run out of hope, you become angry, sad, lonely, and fearful. When you're angry and hungry, you're hangry. You could be hangry for a deeper relationship with your Father God, your Creator. The angry feelings, disappointment, and loneliness you're experiencing are signs of malnourishment, signs you are craving the food that gives you a healthy soul.

Most people aren't feeding their soul enough through reading and relationship. You need these two Rs in order to find your faith and yourself—reading and relationship. You do not have to read the Bible in a year or try to achieve some other written challenge. Like a steak that often needs to be marinated, so does a tough Bible passage. Furthermore, a relationship is not going to be formed overnight. Each day is one more building block that forms the strong relationship on that solid foundation of faith. And honestly, the best relationships are built over time, not hurried along. Fast relationships usually fall away. How many long-term friendships do you have still to this day that took years to build? (Yeah, me too!) "Like newborn babies, crave pure spiritual milk, so that by it you may grow up in your salvation, now that you have tasted that the Lord is good." —1 Peter 2:2–3

THE WORD BECAME FLESH

You are God's temple. Dig inside yourself to see what holds you back from fully surrendering your life to the will of God. You need space for God in your heart. You need to trust that He is the Bread of Life, and you will get everything you need from Him. You'll never go hungry or thirst again.

> Very truly I tell you, the one who believes has eternal life. I am the bread of life. Your ancestors ate the manna in the wilderness, yet they died. But here is the bread that comes down from heaven, which anyone may eat and not die. I am the living bread that came down from heaven. Whoever eats this bread will live forever. This bread is my flesh, which I will give for the life of the world. (John 6:47–51)

Breaking bread is the answer to your brokenness. It was through Jesus's breaking (death) that you are mended (healed). By His wounds you are healed (Isaiah 53:5). His death made it possible for you to reconnect with God—because every barrier was broken. Your connection is just a prayer away. Jesus cures your wounds and feeds your starving soul. When you allow Him to do the mending and feeding, instead of trying to do it yourself, you will feel more satisfied instead of empty.

PRAY FOR YOUR FOOD

George Müller is a powerful example of faith. If you haven't read about him, he exhibited greater faith than most anyone in history. He ran several orphanages in Bristol, England, solely on faith and prayers. He never earned a paycheck and survived without directly asking for donations. That didn't stop the donations from coming or the food from being delivered. His prayers for daily bread were always answered. He's also known for inspirational quotes, like this one: "God delights to increase the faith of His children. We ought, instead of wanting no trials before victory, no exercise for patience, to be willing to take them from God's hand as a means. I say—and say it deliberately—trials, obstacles, difficulties, and sometimes defeats, are the very food of faith."

In eternity, you will always be satisfied and never hungry, but until then you need to keep feeding your body and your soul. Always look to the Bread of Life for your spiritual nourishment and you'll need for nothing else. Find activities or worship that connect you to God and soothe your soul. Don't just ask for needs to be met, read a Christian book, or listen to worship music; engage in things that connect you to your Creator. This can be similar to emotional self-care, but it also builds upon the knowledge that you are loved and created for a purpose.

Assurance of Truth

Most Christians find life to be a messy experience. I have definitely seen it in my life. When life is going good, it's easy to be full of faith and feel content with how my life is going. I often feel confident in my own abilities. But as soon as life gets rough, the storms rage, or there is a disaster, my security starts to waiver and I'm not so sure God is still there or even cares about me. I lose my assurance and I doubt God's promises.

When my firstborn was thirteen months old, she slid her fifteen-pound body through a railing and fell about twelve feet to a brick floor, hitting her head. She wasn't crying when I got to her, just moaning. The emergency number wasn't working, so I picked up her tiny body, holding her neck between my finger and my thumb, and rushed her to my aunt's car after she announced she would drive. We were on the road within minutes of the fall. At the nearby small hospital, I ran past the reception desk, through the waiting room, and into the back, screaming that I needed immediate attention. After they took her, it was then that I collapsed to the floor. I could finally feel the overwhelming fear and uncertainty, in those few short minutes of this ordeal, while doctors and nurses surrounded her. Thankfully, they knew our family, and I didn't have to do anything but melt onto the ground. All I remember them saying is it was a fractured skull and slight brain bleed. Next thing I remember, we were on our way to the nearest children's hospital about an hour away. I sat in the front seat, just watching the speedometer and praying God would make it all go away. It felt like a nightmare. How could He take my one-year-old child? I had dedicated her to the church just ten short months before. I prayed the prayer many of us pray in these sorts of rock bottom moments. *If you save my child, I'll do anything you ask. I'll never do another bad thing again.* I thought I was being punished. I also thought, *If you take my child, you are the cruelest God ever, and I will be very angry at you for a very long time.*

I had been placing conditions like this on God since I was a young child. *If He answers this prayer, I'll do this or not do that. If I get this thing I want, I'll appreciate it and share with others.* But through pain and suffering, I learned that setting up conditions for God to meet or not meet stopped me from worshipping the Lord who deserves my worship. He doesn't place conditions on us.

It's so hard to not believe that being a Christian means life will be perfect, that our faith gives us a guarantee we'll escape the effects of the normal problems all humans face. But perfection is not obtainable. Not only will we not have a perfect life, our faith won't be perfect also. My assurance that God would protect my children from any harm was shaken on that day my daughter fell. I started to realize bad things could happen to my family. Almost fifteen years later, our family was divided in two because of my divorce. Again, my faith was put to the test. It was hard to believe God really wanted good things for me, hard for me to believe I wasn't being punished, even though I wasn't doing anything wrong. But here I am, seven years after my divorce, writing this book about repairing faith while learning how God used my imperfect life to repair my imperfect faith. I have no doubt God has great things in store for me, even while my life is still not perfect. All I can do is stand on the solid foundation of truth and trust His promises.

Side note: My daughter ended up surviving and healing but developed epilepsy as a teen, possibly because of the scar tissue on her brain. Thankfully, as far as I know, she doesn't have any lasting effects from the fall or the complex partial seizures she experienced as a teen.

Going Deeper

READ MARK 9:14–29. DOES ANYTHING STAND OUT?

WRITE 1 THESSALONIANS 1:5.

ASSURANCE: "A positive declaration intended to give confidence; a promise or certainty about something."[13]

SYNONYMS

Assertion, certainty, declaration, edict, insistence, pronouncement

CAN I TRUST IN GOD'S PROMISES?

AM I MAKING ANY DECLARATIONS TO STAND FIRM ON MY FAITH—A GIFT GIVEN TO ME?

DO I NEED TO ASK THE HOLY SPIRIT TO HELP ME WITH MY DOUBT?

Biblically Speaking

All Christians struggle with unbelief at some point because no one can see everything God sees. Humans don't know everything He knows, or how their story will end. Unbelief and faith *can* exist in your mindset at the very same time because you only see what you see with your eyes and nothing more. Brains don't even have all the needed information to be perfect in faith, so people have times of struggle.

In Mark 9, you read about a boy with epilepsy or demon possession (his appropriate diagnosis is often debated by many biblical scholars because of the father's description in Matthew 17). Jesus heard the doubt in the boy's father's voice when he asked *if* Jesus could help. Jesus reminded him anything is possible if the person believes (v. 23). The disciples also lacked faith, and they were walking with the Lord in person. Jesus's scolding was an invitation for them to proclaim with certainty that He was who He said He was. The boy's father then asked for help to overcome his unbelief.

In John 6:47, Jesus used the Greek (originally Aramaic) word *amēn*, or "verily," which means "truly" or "to say He was telling the truth." He is the Bread of Life. "Anyone who eats this bread will live forever" (v. 51). Jesus was giving His assurance that He was sent by God to give eternal life to those who believe and accept Him as their Savior. He mentioned no other requirements or disqualifications beyond belief. You are immediately adopted into His family when you believe. As you learned earlier this week, humans hunger for this bread. Bread is necessary for physical life but Jesus is necessary for eternal life. Jesus was not implying that communion bread is necessary for eternal life but that when you accept Him into yourself, you shall become one flesh with Him. Jesus doesn't fill your belly but fills your soul. You won't feel spiritually hungry when you're filled up with Jesus.

When the storms of life rage, you may feel a lack of faith or unbelief that Jesus is still really who He says He is. Unbelief is not the opposite of faith. Understand that when your faith is being tested and doubt creeps in, this is just another chance to grow in your faith. Ask Him to help you in your unbelief.

> Sanctify them in the truth [set them apart for Your purposes, make them holy]; Your word is truth. (John 17:17 AMP)

SAY AMEN!

When you say amen at the end of a prayer, you're saying you faithfully, truly believe with exclamation! You are assured that God is still on the throne and His will *will* be done. It's a statement to relieve doubt, to remind you to keep your eyes on the good things you can't see, not the fleeting circumstances you're currently in. Instead of doubt, Jesus said to live in confidence that what God says in His Word is truth. Amen?!

> Blessed be the Lord, the God of Israel, From everlasting even to everlasting. And let all the people say, 'Amen.' Praise the Lord! (Hallelujah!) (Psalm 106:48 AMP)

Week 3
I Am Worthy!

YOU, LORD, ARE OUR FATHER. WE ARE
THE CLAY, YOU ARE THE POTTER; WE
ARE ALL THE WORK OF YOUR HAND.
—ISAIAH 64:8

A New Marriage

Although my former husband stated he was a Christian, the day of our wedding proved to me we were unequally yoked. The pastor who married us asked us not to drink before the wedding, but my husband to be did so anyway. During the reception, he was consuming hard liquor with his drinking buddies. Because I was able to keep the promise we had made to each other to stay dry that day, so we'd both remember, I had to drive us home. At that point, the caregiver in me refused to see the lack of maturity and integrity in my new husband. We were both really young, so I guess I just expected it, thinking he'd outgrow this way of living in due time.

Within a month of our wedding date, I found a hookup website in the internet cookie history of our shared computer. Out of curiosity and desperation, I created my own fake profile on this site to see what was really going on. After searching the website, I found his active profile. When he answered my fake profile's invitation to meet, I was furious. That's not what he was supposed to do! He was supposed to get scared he'd hurt his wife and immediately delete his profile and repent. That started my decade-long disappointment and grief at his choice to repeatedly dishonor our marriage vows. And this didn't end until our divorce was finalized in 2013.

After each of his affairs, I wanted him to prove his love and unending devotion to me and only me, but he continued to let me down time and time again. He couldn't love me so I accepted much less than I deserved. I lowered my standards in order to accept whatever he had to offer, when Someone was always willing to give me so much more than I felt I deserved.

While married, my husband was at the center of my life. He relocated our family twice in our marriage—moves across the state of Michigan. I thought it was my duty to follow this man wherever he led. He was in charge of our family, and I was to submit to his ways of running our family—even if that meant into the ground. I didn't realize that not only was he leading our family selfishly, he also wasn't capable of leading our family at all.

During our separation, he told me we would "probably" get back together. As I felt God's love more and more, I knew I could only accept a man of integrity to lead my heart in the future. I was worth this much. That allowed me to let go rather than try to force my will any longer for my marriage. If God wanted me to divorce because I deserved better, then I was willing to accept that. I didn't want to be married to someone without integrity. I could no longer trust my husband to protect my heart. There were no signs of change. I had to start protecting my heart from him! The man who vowed to love, honor, and cherish my heart had damaged it, and our marriage was broken. On the day the divorce was finalized, I was no longer his caretaker, social worker, or probation officer. I was free to breathe again and accept the love of my Creator.

That's when I started to realize God is better than any earthly husband, and I am His bride. I asked to feel His presence and He answered my prayers. He makes me feel special. He's always with me (Matthew 28:20). He will never leave nor forsake me (Hebrews 13:5). God stepped in and proved His love for me and still continues to do so today. This is His nature and it will never change. He wants to be one with all of His children. He seeks to make us His bride. He keeps His promises.

Going Deeper

READ JOHN 17:20–25 AND ISAIAH 54:4–8. DOES ANYTHING STAND OUT?

WRITE JOHN 17:23.

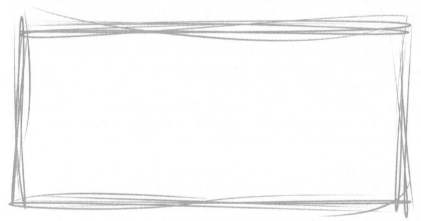

UNITY (BE ONE): "The state of being united or joined as a whole."[14]

SYNONYMS

Attach, connect, integrate, knit together, merge, unify

AM I ONE WITH MY CREATOR?

IS HE MY HUSBAND?

HAVE I ACCEPTED HIS PROPOSAL TO JOIN IN UNION WITH HIM?

HOW CAN I BE MORE UNIFIED WITH THE ONE WHO WAS WILLING TO COME TO EARTH AND DIE FOR ME?

Biblically Speaking

Jesus is love and grace personified. His time in ministry was to not only show the power God had but also His love for His people. During that time, women were treated very poorly, yet Jesus treated them better than anyone had before. Jesus's interactions with women were loving, honoring, and forgiving. He refused to treat them as inferior. He treated them as equals. He had sympathy for the hurting, the injured, the sinful, and the dead. He denied they were unclean and called them healed because of their faith. He rejected the punishment of a woman caught in sin because no one is without sin. Instead, He showed her and others great compassion.

John 17 is Jesus's last will and testament. It is a prayer for the unity of the community of faith and for unity with your heavenly Father and Husband. The same love and glory that was given to Jesus is also available to you. Your oneness with God, this side of heaven, is because of the sacrifice Jesus made on the cross—the greatest love one Man had for His bride, you.

The Hebrew word *echad,* pronounced ekh·äd', means "one." Many times in the Bible, *echad* means simply "one single item." Other times it means "compound unity, many parts coming together into one single entity," for example, the Trinity (God, Son, and Holy Spirit). "But now [at this very moment] in Christ Jesus you who once were [so very] far away [from God] have been brought near by the blood of Christ" (Ephesians 2:13 AMP). When a couple marries, they are to come *yahhad* (together) to become *echad* (one) flesh. Each is to be one flesh together, each contributing one whole of the whole: 1+1=1. When one of the couple is not whole (unhealed and incomplete with God), doesn't "leave and cleave" (Genesis 2:24), or doesn't unite in the covenant, then the couple never really becomes one unit, which could leave the "marriage" vulnerable to the enemy's temptations and/or divorce. They are unequally yoked (2 Corinthians 6:14). Similar to a bicycle with one flat tire, it can never ride smoothly. You need two full tires to ride a bike, just as you need two whole people to create a one-flesh union.

After a breakup or divorce, God calls you and your heart back to Him (v. 6). He sees the grief and wants to heal His creation—His daughter, His bride. Have faith when the unyoking takes place and the covenant with the Lord begins. When you accept the Holy Spirit, you become joined to Him—united as one. One within yourself and one with Him. "This mystery is that through the gospel the Gentiles are heirs together with Israel, members together of one body, and sharers together in the promise in Christ Jesus" (Ephesians 3:6).

The only way to tell a pure, godly heart from an evil heart is to spend time betrothed (attached, committed) to your loving Husband, heavenly Father, and Creator (all fully part of one flesh). You belong to Him. The betrothal gift given to you by Jesus is the Holy Spirit. In His physical absence, the Holy Spirit is your comforter, assuring you of your future inheritance in Christ. He will righteously steward you. He will be the Man you always wished you had and more, fully faithful and always present. Although He'd rather we stay consecrated to Him, God permits remarriage after a time of healing and spiritual growth. In His perfection, He will set up the standards for what you deserve. If or when a new man comes into your life, God will still be your Husband, setting the standards for how you will live as a married couple. But because an earthly man will never be able to fill your every need or the emptiness inside, you must still count on your heavenly Father and Husband to affirm you and give you comfort and purpose.

All the glory will be to God as the One who walks with you through all the trials of your life and in eternity, no matter if you stay single or remarry after divorce.

I Am His Beloved

Before I knew God's love, I internalized everything said about me and to me. These words became my identity as a human being. I based my personal truth and worth on how other people treated me or how they described me. When people in my life, mostly family, said I was an idiot, worthless, and unlovable, I believed them. Their actions of always being too busy for me and having more important things in life to do said loudly that I wasn't important, I couldn't do anything right, and I was always messing up something.

After a breakup with my high school sweetheart, who was the kindest young man I knew, I felt I wasn't deserving of anyone's love. Although he said he didn't want to hurt me, I felt rejected. I internalized his need to go away to college as a single man as being about *me* not being good enough. My thoughts and feelings about myself shaped my beliefs. I was unworthy of the kind of love I had with my first boyfriend. My beliefs directed my actions and led me toward even more poor choices and sinful behaviors. Searching to heal my pain, I looked for love and acceptance anywhere I thought I could get it. I dated pretty much any guy who came along; thankfully, only a handful did. I was pregnant before I was eighteen, with the baby who fractured her skull a little over a year later. The emotionally unavailable father of this beautiful girl wanted no part of our lives. This led to more feelings of unworthiness. I continued to date the angry, uncaring, bad boys of the world. My family kept telling me I would need to take whatever I could get, implying I wasn't good enough for anyone who would treat me right or give me an emotionally healthy relationship (which, honestly, I didn't know I deserved).

That was the story of my life until a couple of years later, after having one more child with a physical abuser. My two daughters, both under the age of two, and I were invited to attend a weekly community dinner night at a local church. I share more of how I learned forgiveness through this church, but it was when I was introduced to Jesus and what He did *for me* on the cross that my heart changed.

At that time, I didn't realize how much my soul was crying out for His acceptance and love. I finally felt acceptance and compassion, something my family of origin was unable to provide. Because of that, the words written on my heart weren't nice: layers and layers of mistreatment, dejection, and shame. I had lived in the world and participated in what the world told me was normal for a teenage girl and young adult. This alone left countless wounds. Then, add in how I thought my own birth family saw me, and I was in need of God's rehabilitation. The rejection wound was so wide and so deep that it would take me years and years, and even a divorce, to get through it all. Like layers of old wallpaper in an old house, I had to peel back each layer and ask God to reveal truth to me. I wasn't an idiot. The Holy Spirit helped me to graduate cum laude from a Christian university. I wasn't unlovable. Jesus loves me enough to die for me. He healed me and put me back on a solid foundation. I wasn't unworthy. God gave me a plan, purpose, and worth. No earthly person can take any of that away with their words or their beliefs.

After I peeled back all of the scars on my heart, I saw the little girl, God's girl, whom the world had destroyed. No one saw the value I possessed as a young child or as a woman. No one told me my life had meaning and purpose. They kicked around my meaningless heart, and so did I, until God took me back from all the people who tried to hurt me. He saw my broken heart and damaged soul and made me whole. Now I guard my healed heart and only share it with those who are trustworthy, honoring, and faithful to God's standards. "Above all else, guard your heart, for everything you do flows from it" (Proverbs 4:23).

After accepting myself as a child of God, I was able to rewrite self-affirming dialogue on my heart, while learning to protect it from future harm. I am His beloved. My heart is precious to Him. Not because of anything I've done or not done correctly because God doesn't see my sin. Jesus washed it white as snow. Instead, He sees me as He sees Jesus, His beloved child, wearing a white robe of honor. Like the prodigal son, I was a wretched sinner who is loved through grace. Like the lost sheep, God searched and pursued me. He knew me inside and out, and He still wanted me and called me His beloved child. When I was far away from Him, He waited for me to come back home to Him with arms wide open.

God is relentless in His pursuit for His beloved children. God is always closer than we realize. And He's always waiting for us to bring Him close and accept His unconditional love.

Going Deeper

READ PSALM 139. DOES ANYTHING STAND OUT?

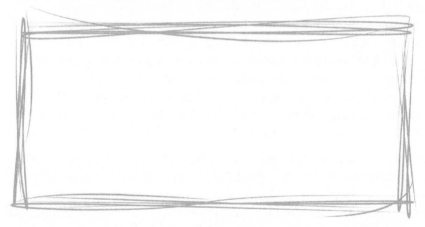

WRITE JEREMIAH 1:5.

KNOWN: "Recognized, familiar, or within the scope of knowledge."[15]

SYNONYMS

Accepted, acknowledged, established, familiar, preferred, recognized

DO I BELIEVE I AM KNOWN, SEEN, AND ACCEPTED BY GOD, EVEN IF MY PAST WASN'T PERFECT?

WHAT TRIGGERS HOLD ME BACK FROM SEEING THE TRUTH ABOUT MYSELF, MY PURPOSE, AND TO WHOM I BELONG?

IN WHAT WAYS CAN I REINFORCE TRUTH TO OVERWRITE THE WORLD'S LIES?

Biblically Speaking

Psalm 139 is summed up in the first sentence of the first verse, "O Lord, you have searched me [thoroughly] and have known me" (AMP). This verse is a reminder that before you pursued Him, He pursued you. Because He knows everything, He's omniscient, and He saw it all, from the moment you were conceived until now. With every little lie or slip of the tongue, He was there watching you with enduring love, knowing one day you'd have a better relationship with Him. Envision that for a minute. You were just living your life but God was watching over you—while you spat out your baby food, threw that temper tantrum, broke up with your first boyfriend, and messed things up or made wrong choices—and He said, "That is my beloved daughter and I'm waiting for her. She's going to come back to me. I'm just waiting for her to finish what she's doing." He has your picture on heaven's refrigerator with the rest of His pictures of His beloved children. He's waiting to wrap you in His comfort and care.

HUMANS NEED TO BE LOVED

All human beings have a biological need to be loved and nurtured. Women feel loved and nurtured when they are known, heard, and understood. You *can* have intimacy without any physical or sexual connection. True intimacy is the emotional connection of being known and fully accepted just as you are; it's when someone deeply loves you despite what they know about you. You are secure when they look at the deepest, darkest parts of you and say, "You are safe with me."

The Greek word *ginosko*, pronounced ge-no'-sko, means "to know and understand completely," which implies an instinctive and deliberate kind of knowledge. Knowledge that is not shared openly and freely with just anyone. It's awareness and familiarity of the private parts of a person. That's why intimacy is often known as a private matter between two lovers. When you share your secrets and your hidden self, you open yourself up to a deeper, more intimate relationship. This is needed for a true, one-flesh connection. God put in your biological need for intimacy before you were born for a reason—so you would run to Him when all other avenues for unconditional love and safe intimacy run out. Because God is love, no one can love you as much as He does. He stands at the bend in the road and waits for you, the prodigal daughter, to come back to Him—to the only love that satisfies.

In the story of the prodigal son (Luke 15), the younger son left his family for what he thought would be a better life out in the world, taking his inheritance with him. When his money ran out, he got to the end of himself and he had no place to stay, but the Father took him back with open arms. It was in that moment He knew the Father's unconditional love. Sometimes humans are just like the prodigal son, walking away from Him and His desire for them. And sometimes humans are like the older brother, bothered when someone else receives grace for all their sins. No matter which brother you've been, God still loves each of His beloved children and bestows His grace and unconditional love upon you.

GOD'S SON

Jesus was His beloved son. God felt joy when He saw His son baptized with the Holy Spirit, accepting the path before Him (Luke 3:22). When Jesus took your punishment for sin on the cross, you became His beloved— greatly loved or dear to the heart. "God demonstrates his own love for us in this: While we were still sinners, Christ died for us" (Romans 5:8). Knowing and accepting God's love are the means to strengthen your faith. Psalm 139 shares how precious you are to Him. You are beloved.

God's love for His people is beyond comprehension. It's easy to hear about it and consciously understand it, but how do you know this in your inner being? The One who knows you inside and out—the good, bad, and everything in between—still loves you in your current condition. He always knows your struggles, your deepest thoughts, and where you are. He never leaves nor forsakes you, even when you're far from Him. He is always waiting with open arms. He wants you to know you are safe, regardless of how you are feeling or what you have done. You are always welcome to nestle back under His wing or lie at His feet. Your identity is in being His beloved. He is your salvation, and He fills your need for belonging. He has a special place for you in His heart, as any loving parent would have. Brendan Manning, in his book *Abba's Child: The Cry of the Heart for Intimate Belonging,* says, "Define yourself radically as one beloved by God. This is the true self. Every other identity is an illusion." When you accept this identity of being worth more than rubies (Psalm 31:10), beloved, you are better able to face your giants—the lies of the enemy and the temptations of this world. You will flee from all unrighteousness. No temptation can overcome you because, just like Jesus, you know who you belong to.

You are known and you are loved. You are His masterpiece. You are worthy! Marinate in those truths today!

God's Masterpiece

When I was younger, I liked to put together puzzles with my grandmother. I recall on one occasion putting together a puzzle with a Thomas Kinkade painting on it. She was going to have the painting glued to a backing and framed to look at for years to come. The pieces were very tiny and had very little detail, and it was so hard and such a slow, tedious process to find which pieces went together, especially if one piece was missing and I had to locate it in the box of unused pieces.

If you've put together large puzzles, you know to start with the outside edges to complete the frame and then work on the middle. And it's not until you have most of the puzzle together that you start to make out the entire picture. Thankfully, with puzzles, we're given the complete picture on the front of the box. Sadly, it's not the same in life. But God sees it all.

He saw my complete picture when I was just a bunch of pieces in a box on the store shelf. In my childhood, I couldn't see why I had to experience the toxic family I was being brought up in, why I got pregnant as a teenager after one sexual encounter, why I married someone who was unfaithful multiple times and made me feel more unworthy of love. These were all pieces to the puzzle of my life, even if I didn't see how they would all fit together. But I've learned God puts them all together to create the masterpiece of my life. Each piece may seem odd shaped, and I've wondered where it fits, but God knows.

For much of my life, I felt I needed to plan everything and get my hands all dirty in trying to create the life I wanted—married by a certain age, own a home by this or that age, and so much more. But my divorce caused me to realize that when I put my hands on things, I can make a big mess of my life. Now, in my middle age, the picture is becoming clearer. I needed to experience what I've experienced. I'm able to educate other women about toxic families and marriages because of what I've been through. Every experience has been given a new meaning—not to hurt me but to help others. That's why I still believe my life verse is Genesis 50:20: "You intended to harm me, but God intended it for good to accomplish what is now being done, the saving of many lives."

I needed to struggle with writing in college so I would take a course with a teacher who would tell me I should start writing online, which is when I started my blog. She helped me write my (unpublished) first book, a children's book about the life of Joseph, son of Jacob—one of my favorite stories.

> The story of Joseph is in the Bible for this reason: to teach you to trust God to trump evil. What Satan intends for evil, God, the Master Weaver and Master Builder, redeems for good. (Max Lucado, *You'll Get Through This: Hope and Help for Your Turbulent Times*)

People poured manure on my life and it helped fertilize God's soil. God planted the seeds of ministry in my mind before I even divorced. I already had a popular homeschool blog, which I turned into a divorce healing blog after my divorce. I'm taking all of the pieces, pulling them together into this Bible study you can use to strength your faith and regain yourself after divorce. That's a beautiful masterpiece—both mine and yours—and I'm so glad God is using mine to help you.

I believe everything, even all the bad, has been used to shape me into who I am. Without a piece, I would be missing something I would need to make me whole and complete as God's masterpiece. You may not start a ministry or write a book after your divorce, but your half-completed masterpiece can and will be used for a bigger purpose as well. It will be a showpiece for someone else who needs to hear it. If for some reason you feel you can't share your masterpiece with the world, hand someone a copy of this book and tell them you were healed by the healing power of Jesus, and now they can be too. Or just start a Bible study group in your community. Either way, you're sharing your pieces with the world.

Going Deeper

READ EPHESIANS 2. DOES ANYTHING STAND OUT?

WRITE EPHESIANS 2:10.

MASTERPIECE: "A work done with extraordinary skill; especially: a supreme intellectual or artistic achievement."[16]

SYNONYMS

Classic, gem, flower, jewel, showpiece, treasure,

CAN I SEE HOW MY LIFE IS BEING KNIT TOGETHER, PIECE BY PIECE?

WHAT ODD OR HARD THINGS HAVE HAPPENED IN MY LIFE THAT ARE HELPFUL TO ME OR TO OTHERS, NOW OR IN THE FUTURE?

Biblically Speaking

Artists spend years or decades studying their craft. They learn proper technique and practice each one over and over until they create their first and sometimes only masterpiece. That piece is the best of the best. It's usually put on display, and someone might pay top dollar to purchase it. After the artist's death, it's worth even more because the artist cannot create another just like it.

God created the sun, the moon, mountains, trees, flowers, and everything on earth—and He said it was good. Then He created you and said you were His one-of-a-kind masterpiece. When God creates each and every person, He does so like He's creating a work of art to glue together, frame, and admire. The odd-shaped pieces of your puzzle will all eventually fit together to make God's greatest achievement, the classic that you are. You are His work of art, the best of the best. He cannot make another one like you. You and all your imperfections, all the things you hate about yourself, and all your mistakes and missteps are just parts of the bigger picture called your life. Yes, you, including all of that stuff, are a masterpiece! Your feelings or your inner dialogue might tell you something different, but feelings can deceive you. They lie! You might think you're a work in process, but God sees you as perfect, even while He works out the rough spots and adds more pieces. Seeing yourself through His eyes helps you to accept your position in the kingdom of God. His feelings for you are always true and never, ever change.

Every night around the world, people experience a beautiful sunset with colors and décor that leave the viewer in awe. As the days and the years pass, this sunset changes but never gets old. No matter how many times you look at one, it takes your breath away again. This is how God sees you, His priceless piece of art, His beautiful masterpiece. You are a gem, beautiful flower, jewel, and showpiece created by Him and for Him. God was there with you in the womb. He saw every cell, every birthmark, every dimple, every freckle while it was being created. He can count every hair on your head like an artist counts brushstrokes. Just as you feel love at the sight of a newborn baby, God sees you the very same way, every single day of your life, no matter your age.

> You are a masterpiece. A painting. A poem. A song. A statue. A work of art. Think of yourself that way. Embrace yourself that way. Honor yourself that way. In doing so you are honoring Him who made you. But you don't feel like a masterpiece. That's ok because I'm not talking about your emotions. I'm talking about you. Those feelings are real, but in a sense, they are irrelevant because they don't change the facts. You are a masterpiece whether you feel like one or not. You may feel like a failure, but God says you are his workmanship, created in Christ Jesus for good works. That's the reality you need to focus on when your feelings tell you something else. God will raise your feelings up to your destiny, don't lower your destiny down to your feelings. (Tony Evans)

Jesus gave you a spiritual life and made you part of Him—a masterpiece. You have a kingdom purpose, planned for you long ago, and it's about time you accept this royal position. His beloved, His masterpiece—you are worthy!

The Daughter of a King

While I was going through my divorce, the women's Bible study at the church I was attending was working through *Anointed, Transformed, Redeemed: A Study of David* (by Beth Moore, Kay Arthur, and Priscilla Shirer). The study walked through the life of David from before he was anointed to be king all the way through the generational curses (the sword) that plagued his home. Although I was not the one committing adultery or murdering anyone, I could see some parallels of David's life and mine. He was told he would be king and then he had to wait another twenty years to see the fulfillment of the anointing promise. David was even chased away and his life threatened by the current king, Saul, yet, he continued to trust God for protection and the promise of his future life.

Soon after I started this study, I kept receiving a vision of myself on a big stage, speaking to a very large crowd. Although I'm not described as shy, I am introverted, and I would never purposely wish to be on a stage preaching to any kind of audience of more than a handful. Even though I seem confident on my YouTube channel, it took me an entire year after starting my channel to get up the nerve to post my first video. Even then, it took another three years to feel somewhat confident in my abilities. During that women's Bible study, I knew God was saying, "I anointed you long ago for a purpose, and I am taking over as your Shepherd to bring about this purpose." I could feel these visions I was having were part of it, even if all the pieces hadn't been placed together yet, and it wouldn't happen overnight. I had to seek out the next steps He had planned for me and wait patiently for things to be put in place. I cautiously took steps in that direction and then waited to see what would happen next.

At all points on this journey, He has only been the lamp beneath my feet. In the years since that study and my divorce, my close, trustworthy friends spoke words of prophecy to me. They told me I was chosen and that God had a plan. Strangers told me they envisioned me on a stage preaching and teaching someday—again, not something I wanted for myself. But until then I had to earn money to pay the bills; money didn't just fall from the sky like manna. So I started working for another blogger online, tutoring kids in my home, and working part-time jobs here and there while typing away and writing on my own blog and my books.

Is this God's plan and purpose? I've often thought at the end of another rough day at my job. *I thought I was anointed for so much more than this.* Every year I felt like God was taking me down another wrong path. *What does this job have to do with my anointing?* Or *Maybe I'm not listening hard enough to hear what He would have me do.* It was a struggle to know if I was on the right path. I still question at times, even as I write this book: *Is this what I'm supposed to be doing right now? Or should I go get a full-time "real job" as my critics often suggest.*

God knows what's in my heart. I've had a heart for ministry that He placed upon my heart when my (former) husband and two children sat in a new church just a year before we divorced. When we got home, I told my husband I felt God wanted us to go into ministry. I wasn't sure what that looked like at that point, but I felt the pull on my heart to go in that direction. I knew it was something I needed to do. That's when my husband boldly and angrily announced that if this were true for me, we'd have to divorce because he didn't hear God saying that to him. I wonder if my Father in heaven had said, "I need to take my daughter back so she can fulfill her purpose." God saw what was going on behind the scene that I knew nothing about at the time, and He said "If he's not going to support her, I will." After discovering that secret girlfriend shortly after, we were divorced about a year and a half later. God indeed took me back from my grief and became my supportive Husband.

If it weren't for my divorce, I would not be doing what I am doing today. I might be writing books or Bible studies, but they wouldn't be for divorced women. I may not have written any books. I would not be seeking speaking engagements, and I would not be sharing my freedom from this dysfunction. I could not do God's will because I was too busy doing the will of my husband, being a submissive wife, and putting a human at the center of my life. My Father wanted to see me thrive, and slowly, over the last seven years, I've grown in my faith, I've walked in my purpose, and I've accepted that I am the daughter of a King—adopted, worthy, and His beloved. You are too.

Going Deeper

READ GALATIANS 3:23–29. DOES ANYTHING STAND OUT?

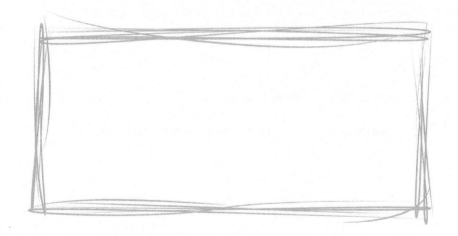

WRITE GALATIANS 3:26.

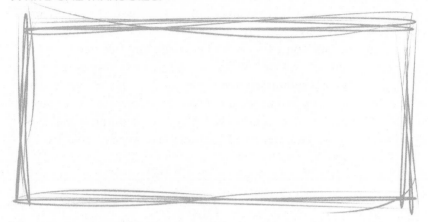

CHILD: "The descendants of a family or people."[17]

DAUGHTER: "Female descendant (Genesis 26:34); A woman (Mark 5:34); Worshipper or group of worshippers of the true God (Zechariah 2:10; Matthew 21:5)."[18]

SYNONYMS

Babe, innocent, minor, offspring, progeny, youth

DO I FEEL UNCONDITIONAL LOVE FROM MY HEAVENLY FATHER AS HIS PRECIOUS CHILD?

I Am Worthy!

HAVE I ACCEPTED MYSELF AS HIS PRECIOUS DAUGHTER?

WHAT DO I NEED TO TELL MYSELF SO I REMEMBER WHO I BELONG TO?

Biblically Speaking

Before Jesus, God's people were subject to the Law of Moses, also known as the Mosaic Law. These laws start with the Ten Commandments and continue throughout the Torah—the first five books of the Bible—including many rules pertaining to religious observances, rituals, and everyday life for the Jewish people. Jesus came to free God's people from this law. There is no more working to be a child of God; His people are one with Him through their faith. All who have faith in Jesus Christ, the Son of Man, and know what He did for them on the cross, are called His sons and daughters. "I will be a Father to you, and you will be my sons and daughters, says the Lord Almighty" (2 Corinthians 6:18).

You have to believe God's love is more powerful than your feelings of insecurity and lack of worth. That's when you'll be on the path to changing how you see yourself. It's not self-esteem that will support you but "God-esteem." You are placed into a royal position (Esther 4:14) because of who your Father is. Your Father is the one true King. His kingdom is heaven, which will live for eternity.

"Yet to all who did receive him, to those who believed in his name, he gave the right to become children of God—children born not of natural descent, nor of human decision or a husband's will, but born of God" (John 1:12–13). You were never orphaned. You are chosen and adopted—born again into God's family. As Jesus called Him, God is the *Abba*, an Aramaic word meaning "daddy," and a term used to talk about God's nature and care for His children. It's a term of endearment. Love is God's nature. The Father delights in His children. "He chose us in him before the creation of the world to be holy and blameless in his sight. In love he predestined us for adoption to sonship through Jesus Christ, in accordance with his pleasure and will—to the praise of his glorious grace, which he has freely given us in the One he loves" (Ephesians 1:5).

Knowing who you are changes your face, the person you see in the mirror, the vision through your own eyes. Your earthly parents gave you a name upon birth, but God gave you a new name upon your second birth as His child—when you accepted Him as your heavenly Father. Through Jesus, God's eyes see your new name, child of the King of all Kings. You are His daughter.

"They will wage war against the Lamb, but the Lamb will triumph over them because he is Lord of lords and King of kings—and with him will be his called, chosen and faithful followers" (Revelation 17:14). Faith is the constant trust in your Father-daughter relationship with Him. It is the deep knowledge of His heart as your provider, protector, and counselor. You were born to be known for what He has done. This is your divine destiny. Now, go out and show the world who you belong to. There is no need to hold anything back.

> Among God's churches we boast about your perseverance and faith in all the persecutions and trials you are enduring. All this is evidence that God's judgment is right, and as a result you will be counted worthy of the kingdom of God, for which you are suffering. (2 Thessalonians 1:4–5)

Don't get stuck in the baby phase. Grow up in your faith and accept the gift you've been given as His daughter. Faith needs to keep growing and maturing, and in time your struggles and times of trials will have no power over you or your feelings. God's nature never changes, even if your circumstances do. Trust in His unchanging nature, in your position in His life, and in the relationship He has with you rather than what you're experiencing. Your faith has made you well. Now you can live in peace, precious daughter!

Created by Design

Growing up, I was often told that I needed to shut up. I grew up with family who believed children should not be seen or heard; we were to go to the basement and be quiet at all family gatherings. I can only think of two people who didn't tell me how mouthy I was on a regular basis. It wasn't that I was disrespectful; I just talked a lot, even in my sleep, despite being an introvert. This is how God created me. And much like my own children, I was a strong-willed child, many times bossy to my cousins and a natural teacher. I played school a lot as a child. I was always the instructor, always in charge, always knowing how things should go.

When I was in the fifth grade, my male teacher thought creative writing was an important skill to learn, so we wrote in our journals every single day. Mr. Glaser was the coolest teacher ever! But I wasn't a great reader and had to go to a special class for those who were behind in their reading. Because of that, I missed writing some days during the week. In high school an English teacher told me I was a horrible writer for my report on *A Tale of Two Cities*. Thinking back now, I didn't enjoy that book at all. I don't think she meant to leave a scar, but reading fiction books bore me to death, so I never really understood the topic I was supposed to be writing about. Because of all those early experiences, my inner dialogue was that I was not a great reader or writer, so it was better to keep away from both. I did for a very long time. I also always tried to keep my mouth shut so no one would notice how mouthy or bossy I was. In my early adulthood, and even sometimes still today, I have to remind myself to not talk so much and to let others talk so I can be a more active listener and learn from the other leaders and instructors of this world.

In 2008, after completing my associate's degree with pretty good grades, I had to submit a writing sample to be admitted to my university's Bachelor of Science program. They let me know right away, after my acceptance to the school and program, that I would need a writing tutor, since much of the work in the program was writing critical thinking essays. Again, a reminder that I wasn't good at writing. I wondered how I'd make it through the program. Thankfully, this writing tutor had a skill so many in my past didn't possess—the ability to pour encouragement and empowerment into me. Like my fifth grade teacher before him, he told me I could do this, that all I needed was practice. He gave me exercises along with compliments that propelled me to keep moving forward. I didn't need to give up or accept the past descriptions of me because he gave me new hope for a better future. Maybe it was my hungry soul, but I enjoyed working with him to improve in my writing abilities. He also encouraged me to take an elective writing course to keep practicing, and it was that university teacher who suggested I start a blog, which was a fairly new thing at that time. Now on my fifth website, God has shown me His plan for me to save many lives by writing books and speaking, which is something I never envisioned for myself back in those difficult years of my childhood. This once mouthy girl—who wouldn't shut up and couldn't read or write very well—and who was criticized for spelling lettuce and yogurt with an "e" instead of a "u" on my grocery list while married, was going to have all these things used for her divine purpose. Who would've thought?

His design, the way He created me, laid out the steps. The disappointments and the encouragements added depth to my call. I needed to marry and divorce and to put Him back into the place He belonged in my life. I even had to lose most of my family to feel I could "run my mouth" on the internet and not have to hear them telling me to stop or shut up. And my strong will and determination help me to ignore those who still try to shut me up to this day. I know I was created for such a time as this.

I don't do this work for my critics. I do it because this is what I was designed to do. I now know my early life helped to make me into what I am today, helping to shape the purpose I live for. The pieces were laid down in my life's bigger picture, and this is what God's masterpiece looks like.

Going Deeper

READ ROMANS 9. DOES ANYTHING STAND OUT?

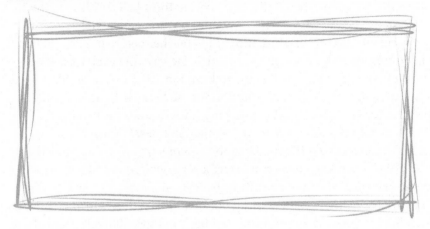

WRITE GENESIS 1:27.

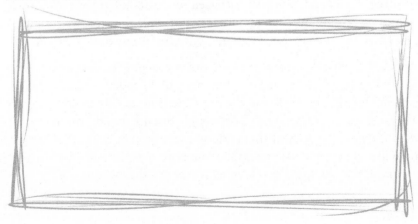

CREATED: "To cause to come into being, as something unique that would not naturally evolve or that is not made by ordinary processes."[19]

SYNONYMS

Design, establish, fabricate, form, organize, shape

AM I ABLE TO BE EVERYTHING GOD CREATED ME TO BE?

WHAT HOLDS ME BACK FROM ACCEPTING MYSELF AS GOD'S DESIGN, HIS MASTERPIECE, TO BE USED FOR A PURPOSE?

CAN I SEE HOW THE BAD THINGS THAT HAVE HAPPENED MAY HAVE HAD A BIGGER PURPOSE?

Biblically Speaking

Architects and contractors who build houses from scratch think about who will be living in the home and about what that family will need before starting the project. What will be the purpose of the building? How many bedrooms and bathrooms will they need? Will they need room for entertaining or a home office? Often, they let the homeowners pick out their own design colors so they really love the place once they're living there. The builders could be selfish and just create a beautiful home without a purpose, but what benefit would that bring to anyone else? Without a room to sleep in, kitchen to cook a meal in, or spaces to store the homeowner's belongings, you'd find it wasn't the perfect home for the family and they'd look for something more suitable. They need rooms this building wouldn't offer.

Thankfully, God is not building homes. He's creating lives with purpose. When God creates someone or something, He not only thinks about what this creation's benefit will be to the world but also what this creation needs to benefit itself. He gives mercy to His created as they grow and mature in Him. You weren't created to merely live or just survive in this world, or to gain something for yourself, but to enhance the world with the uniqueness only you can offer. You are the perfect structure for the purpose you were designed for, no matter how you don't fit into the box the world tries to fit you into.

You were created with the exact fabric God knew you needed to have to be you. Your gender, your personality, the biological family or upbringing that shaped you, as well as the positive and negative influences were all part of creating the unique you. Your creation wasn't some random set of explosions because God formed your DNA and every cell and every molecule. God took the time to design the very complex idea of you, and then He placed you in the exact environment you needed to grow into the version He created you to be and who you are today.

He's not surprised when you do or say something because He knows how you'll be, how He created you to be. Since God doesn't make mistakes, that thing about you you don't like is not a mistake. It's not random. His perfect design, with all the right ingredients measured before you were born, were put into their places for the person He wants and knows is needed in this world. This is what He calls your divine purpose.

> Life in God is not just about having faith in Him. Did you know that He has faith in you too? He is utterly convinced that you are going to be wonderful, exceptional, and brilliant as his child. And He is intentional about changing your perception of yourself to align with His. (Graham Cooke, *Kingdom Thinking Collection*)

You may be wondering how God could have a kingdom purpose for you when you're barely surviving this season of your life. Living a life of faith is trusting that whatever you may be experiencing is all part of that divine purpose, tiny pieces of the puzzle, a part of the bigger picture you were created for. This is no accident because it's part of your unique blueprint.

God created you at the exact moment you were meant to be alive. He saw you as a gift, His precious daughter, His masterpiece, and He said you were not just good but *beloved*. As you grow in your faith, you'll understand everything that has gone into making you, you'll use your unique set of gifts, and the vision for your purpose will become clear. It won't happen overnight, but it will happen. Then you get to decide what to do with it. He wants you to give it back to Him. Are you willing to use yourself as a gift to God and His kingdom? You are a gift to Him, created by design.

Week 4
A Woman of Fearless Faith
(#SquadGoals)

THE LORD IS GOOD, A REFUGE IN TIMES
OF TROUBLE. HE CARES FOR THOSE
WHO TRUST IN HIM.
—NAHUM 1:7

Provided for (Hagar)

I moved out of my mother's home, for the final time, when I was nineteen years old. I was able to get my own apartment because I had a factory job that paid quite well, but I soon found it hard to juggle college and work full time. I moved around a little bit from rental to rental until I lost a job and could no longer pay my rent. I was homeless with nowhere to go. My mother opened up her home to me with a catch. I could only stay there for thirty days and find a job. I had to get out before the end of that time limit. Thanks to the church I had just started attending and their mentoring program, I was taught how to create and keep a budget and quickly got back on my feet with no help from my mother. I was out within the thirty days.

A couple of years later, just when I was about to build my first home through a program for single mothers, I reconciled with an old boyfriend and we decided to get married—my first and only marriage thus far. He moved me away from my support system and the church community to be closer to his family. At the time I thought that was a great idea since I didn't have a lot of family in my life and I was willing to embrace his. Sadly, they could never embrace me in return, which caused a lot of stress on our marriage (besides the other issues). After that, I just assumed he'd always financially take care of me, so I didn't need to worry about money anymore. For the most part, we were taken care of, but there were times when he would use the money to control me or to try to hurt me (financial abuse). And then my divorce became the catalyst for my fear or faith battle—all about money. Maybe it is yours too?

When I share God's promises for providence, protection, and restoration, I often hear, "I hope so!" I, too, have wondered if God would *really* provide for me after my divorce. *What if I am being punished? What happens when child support runs out or just stops unexpectedly, which it has three times?! Will God really keep His promises or will I be homeless? Will we always have to count our pennies and budget for every little thing, or will God provide abundance one day?*

Even when I worry, even when I doubt, I have to recall God's promises. I can be impatient and take matters into my own hands or I can wait to see what God has planned. Although I'd been homeless before I was a Christian, God still took care of me. He still put people in the right places to make sure I never slept on the street or in my car. When I am stressed, I recall all of the times God came through on His promises. He was often there at the last minute, past my comfort zone limit, and long past fear and anxiety that something bad would happen, but He always came through. My hope remains deeply rooted in Him because He's never let me down.

It's not easy to wait for things to get better or for promises to be fulfilled. I often cry out to God for some relief from my current circumstances. While I wait, I keep my eyes on Jesus and learn how to endure and have patience. My character is being smoothed out so I am more like Him. It strengthens my faith.

Going Deeper

READ GENESIS 16; 21:8–20. DOES ANYTHING STAND OUT?

WRITE 2 CORINTHIANS 9:8.

ABUNDANTLY: "In large quantities; plentifully."[20]

SYNONYMS

Amply, bountifully, charitably, freely, plentifully, sufficiently

DO I HAVE THE ASSURANCE I WILL BE PROVIDED FOR, NO MATTER WHAT HAPPENS IN MY LIFE?

WHAT HOLDS ME BACK FROM BELIEVING IN HIS AMPLE PROVISION?

Biblically Speaking

Hagar was a young Egyptian handmaid whose Hebrew name meant "stranger" or "the resident alien." Some believe this was a name given to her by her masters, (Abram) Abraham and (Sarai) Sarah. Hagar was either a present from the pharaoh when the family was in Egypt or acquired at an earlier time. She had converted from her idol-worshipping heritage to follow Abraham's God.[21] The word for slave in Hebrew has the same meaning as "bodies" or "subjects." Hagar was just a body to Sarah with no other purpose than to do what she was told. In Sarah's mind Hagar had no rights. Hagar was in bondage to Abraham and Sarah's choices.

Sarah told Hagar to be a surrogate for the promised heir after Sarah became impatient and doubted God's promises and decided to take matters into her own hands. At that time, it was actually customary for a slave to be purchased just to provide an heir for an infertile couple, but Hagar was already theirs. Abraham viewed her as a second wife, which caused Sarah, embroiled in jealously, to try to take back the upper hand as a Jew in a higher social class than Hagar. Sarah's anger led her to abuse her handmaid.

Abraham and Sarah wanted this child, Ishmael, to be their full heir, but Sarah's jealousy of Hagar created a bad family environment in which to raise a child. Hagar became arrogant and asserted her rights as Abraham's second wife after she became pregnant, which she had every right to do. Secretly, Hagar no longer saw Sarah as her superior and looked with contempt on her mistress. She welcomed herself as the second wife, just as Abraham did. And Abraham abused his power as well. Through it all, Hagar was a strong woman who refused to conform to the role of slave, especially since she was the only one who had a child with Abraham, something Sarah was unable to do. Hagar didn't choose her life, but she knew having this child gave her equality as a wife. She was valuable because she had a divine purpose to produce Abraham's heir.

In her distress at the way Sarah was treating her, Hagar ran away from the family. It was there she met God's angel, who told her her child would be just as strong-willed as she was and would not be domesticated. God saw her humiliation and despair. She was also given the same promise Adam received of too many descendants to count (Genesis 16:10). These promises gave her the strength to continue being a slave to her jealous and abusive mistress—one of those times when people choose the lesser of two evils, knowing that is where God wants them to be for a season.

Side note: This is not to mean any woman should stay in an abusive marriage just to save the marriage or provide for the children. In this case, Hagar's only option for income as a slave was to be a slave for another family, which probably wouldn't have happened given she already had a child, or be a prostitute. For Hagar, it was better to stay than to try things on her own. Nowadays, women have many more options for life after divorce.

Ishmael was fourteen years old when Isaac, the promised heir, was finally born to Sarah. More insecurity caused Sarah to demand that Abraham write Hagar a bill of divorce and send her away to live in the desert. In his confusion and distress, he was unsure what to do until God told him to listen to Sarah. While in the desert, God came to Hagar again, reminding her of His promises to her. God heard her cries and provided what they needed: food, water, and shelter. He supported them and stayed with them in the wilderness. "The eyes of the Lord are on the righteous, and his ears are attentive to their cry" (Psalm 34:15). As a woman without a husband, Hagar experienced prejudice, injustice, abuse, and despair. She was oppressed and rejected by her host family and, ultimately, by her only earthly husband. But God still saw her and heard Ishmael's cries for water. He stepped in as her Lord and Husband. She called Him "the God who sees me." She witnessed the God who sees.

Hagar's story is a reminder that God sees the abuse you endured, sees your needs, and cares for you and your children. He is with you even in the wilderness. Hagar survived and persevered; you will too.

> Do not worry, saying, "What shall we eat?" or "What shall we drink?" or "What shall we wear?" For the pagans run after all these things, and your heavenly Father knows that you need them. But seek first His kingdom and his righteousness, and all these things will be given to you as well. (Matthew 6:31–33)

God was there when Hagar was being abused, when she was feeling lonely, when they were thirsty, and while she was raising her rebellious child. He was there writing her restoration story. He still is today. This time, you are His main character. He sees you!

Redeemed (Rahab)

I have this reoccurring dream where a tall, dark, human figure is standing over me while I sleep. I often wake up with a pillow in my hand, swinging it around wildly toward the open space next to my bed. My teenage son has even heard me yelling, "Get out!" The first few times I experienced this dream, I was a little worried someone might be in our home. When it recurred, I turned on all the lights and searched the entire house, gripping my baseball bat, only to learn no one else was there. Over time I came to understand it just was a recurring dream and I had nothing to fear. "The Lord is my light and my salvation—whom shall I fear? The Lord is the stronghold of my life—of whom shall I be afraid?" (Psalm 27:1). It's not that I never feel fear. I do. I've just learned that because of who I belong to, death and darkness are not such a scary thing. Although I know I am protected, I'm willing to die if that's God's will for my life. As I've learned the nature of God, I know He wouldn't allow anything to happen unless He was going to bring good from it, if there wasn't a greater purpose.

I often wonder if I'm still subconsciously fighting the dark figure of my ex-husband or even my own past sins, fighting all the unresolved issues and the feeling that I'll never see justice for all that has happened, and all that continues to happen, with my children. God knows my heart and knows how I struggle with anger and bitterness at times. Truth be known, I'm jaded after all I've lived through. I have a hard time trusting that good things will happen in my life, even if deep down I know they will.

One of my favorite verses from C. S. Lewis's book *The Problem of Pain* is: "We are not necessarily doubting that God will do the best for us; we are wondering how painful the best will turn out to be." I often feel that things only seem to get worse rather than better. I think about the fact that not only have I lost my marriage but also a couple of my children to after-divorce estrangement as well. Will God redeem my story? What will that look like? Will I be reunited with my adult children? Will I find earthly love again? If I do, will I be able to trust that man, or will he cheat and abuse me too? Will that marriage end in divorce? Have the sins of my past, before I was married and before I was a Christian, tarnished me for life? These are all questions many women in my shoes ask. It's common to wonder if I will go on to have a better life after all I've been through.

While I wonder, I just have to trust that God has bought me back from my toxic marriage for a reason. I have a greater purpose, like many sinners and heroines in Bible history. He plans to not only redeem my story but to also restore what was lost. I only have to learn to be faithfully patient and endure, trusting it's for the best. My having to wait for the redemption story I crave to tell doesn't mean it's not coming. In the meantime, I have this struggling story to tell, just like the many "struggle stories" in the Bible. I am using courage to share my current situation as I wait for the rest of the pieces of my life's puzzle, His masterpiece, to fall into place.

Going Deeper

READ JOSHUA 2 AND 6:22. DOES ANYTHING STAND OUT?

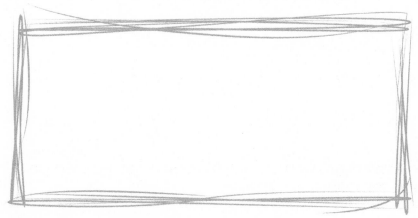

WRITE PSALM 49:5, 7–8, 15.

REDEEM: "To buy back; to recover; to convert."[22]

SYNONYMS

Absolve, acquit, defray, reclaim, regain, save

HAS GOD BOUGHT ME BACK OR ABSOLVED MY SIN?

IN WHAT WAYS HAS GOD REDEEMED MY STORY AND HOW WOULD I LOVE TO SEE HIM REDEEM MORE?

AM I SHOWING THAT I'M SERVING HIM WHILE I WAIT, THROUGH MY WORKS AND COMPASSION FOR OTHERS?

Biblically Speaking

Rahab had incredible courage in the face of danger and even death. She could've been killed for hiding spies in her home yet she believed these men would protect her and her family from harm. She believed in God's protection and providence as well, even after all she had been doing in her life. She had no doubt. She professed her belief that God was the only God when she said, "For the Lord your God is God in heaven above and on the earth below" (Joshua 2:11). In that instance, she was saved. To many this is scandalous. A harlot, or what we call a prostitute today—she hosted and entertained men for a living—was the first to be forgiven and saved by God. How could God forgive and not punish this woman for what she was doing?

Rahab knew God was giving the Israelites power to defeat armies and protection. She wanted in on that. She wanted to save her family. She knew they had a future; there was more to her life than her past. She went from sinner to saved because of her faith in the one true God. She is known as a heroine of faith. Her renowned title came from the fact that she was the first gentile convert. Through God's grace and mercy, she used both faith and works to make her profession of faith on that day.

Jericho followed a pagan culture of idol worship, so Rahab knew about gods. She saw the Jewish God as the one true God, not just another pagan god. Through saving her and her family, God revealed Himself to her. Seeds had been planned, and when she encountered the Israelites, she professed her faith. "In the same way, was not even Rahab the prostitute considered righteous for what she did when she gave lodging to the spies and sent them off in a different direction?" (James 2:25). Rahab lived at a time when all control belonged to men. Patriarchy meant women didn't have rights or freedom. She wasn't so much a sinful woman as she was sinned against—used by men. As a prostitute, she was considered one of the worst sinners, yet her actions and beliefs made her a legit bride, washed white as snow.

Even after being saved, her name *Rahab* would always show her sin. Her name means "broad (wide)" and "fierceness (menacingly wild)." She was probably treated as a moral leper with a name like that. But that was a season of her life she left behind. She was saved by grace, so her past no longer mattered. God saw her as a heroine of faith. After the destruction of Jericho, she married an Israelite named Salmon and they had a child, Boaz, Ruth's second husband and the great-grandfather of David. "His father Zechariah was filled with the Holy Spirit and prophesied: 'Praise be to the Lord, the God of Israel because he has come to his people and redeemed them. He has raised up a horn of salvation for us in the house of his servant David'" (Luke 1:67–69).

When Rahab needed protection and saving, she didn't shy away from asking for what she needed for herself and her family. She protected the spies and they made a promise to save her in return. She became one of them. Her transformation was a paragon of hospitality, mercy, patience, repentance, and faith. She was spared in Jericho to be yet another example of God's lovingkindness and grace for the downtrodden of this world. It was through faith she was saved. Her purpose was to be a part of God's plan, part of "His-story." It was long after her death that her life became most meaningful in the kingdom of God. She walked into eternity before the self-righteous of that time, knowing God's mercy is available for even the vilest of sinners. Faith radiates from those we least expect, those with the biggest sins and the biggest struggles. The prostitute was redeemed. God chose Rahab. He bought her by paying for her sin with His life and included her in Christ's family tree.

God was there in Rahab's story. He is there for yours. Rahab was given a new life with the Lord and became a beloved daughter. You are too! What a woman! What a purpose! Now it's your turn.

Restored (Ruth + Naomi)

I am still dealing with the aftermath of my divorce destruction. I'm bitter. I don't like some of the things I have had to deal with, all the losses. I still love God and trust Him, but I've been in this cleanup season for seven years. I'm tired! Although I know it will end, I'm weary, as I know it won't end tomorrow or next week.

Ever since my divorce, I've been in this season of singleness and estrangement from two children while raising an emotionally hurting child. Unlike my other two children, my youngest has taken the divorce the hardest. Most days he's angry. In the beginning, he just wanted to have his family back together. It would not and could not be that way. He internalizes his pain and grief over the losses. As the days and years go by, I am starting to see what God was protecting us from. He gives us all free will, and when someone turns down a path of sin, with no conscience for repentance, He needs to remove His children from that environment. In God's lovingkindness for my child and myself, He needed to remove us from the destruction we called family.

"If anyone causes one of these little ones—those who believe in me—to stumble, it would be better for them to have a large millstone hung around their neck and to be drowned in the depths of the sea" (Matthew 18:6). God has tasked me, in this season, to stop the cycle of abandonment and abuse.

I wasn't able to see the need for this until after I was clear that was what we were dealing with. I needed to get out of the situation to see and understand it fully. It's a generational curse that is trying to harm my children too, but through God's strength and my faith, I have hope in the power of a mother's prayer for her legacy.

I wish I could see past the tree to the entire forest. I wish I could get a glimpse of the masterpiece God is creating, either in me or my children. Instead, all I see is what is right before me, what I'm experiencing. I tell this to God and He understands my angst and desperation for things to change, just as Naomi did after her husband and sons died (Ruth 1). I know that one day all of this, even my children's lives, will be restored. I'm learning to have quiet patience while I endure. Ruth and Naomi are two great reminders that God is working behind the scenes, figuring out the details, even when we cannot see it. I can't see what God has planned for the future, but I can trust it's all for good. The story of Ruth and Naomi is one of my favorites. I know; I have a lot. I enjoy Bible history. I know God's lovingkindness for His precious daughters! I know He wants me to remain faithful, trust, and follow wherever He leads me. I'm walking in the desert and doing what He asks. I work and He provides everything we need. In return, He accepts my season of bitterness as right where I am on this divorce-healing journey. Like Naomi, I hope to have my heart warmed when I see whatever God has planned to restore my life in the future.

Going Deeper

READ RUTH 4. DOES ANYTHING STAND OUT?

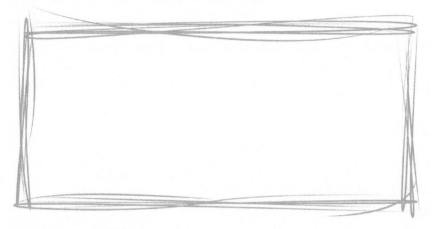

WRITE 1 PETER 5:10.

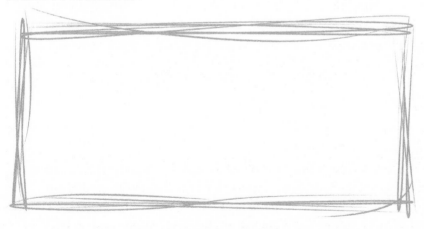

RESTORE: "To mend, to furnish completely."[23]

SYNONYMS

Cure, improve, rebuild, rehabilitate, repair, strengthen,

IN WHAT WAYS DO I NEED GOD'S STRENGTH AND JESUS'S HEALING WHILE WAITING FOR HIS PROMISED RESTORATION AND REDEMPTION?

PRAY AND ASK HIM FOR EVERYTHING YOU NEED—EVEN YOUR HEART'S DESIRES. HE PROVIDES!

Biblically Speaking

Ruth's name meant "something worth seeing and female friend." She was a kind woman with both interior and exterior beauty. Ruth started out empty-handed when she accompanied Naomi back to her homeland but ended up fully restored and redeemed. "Redeem" means to "buy back" or "win back something that was lost." God buys back His daughters from their broken marriages in order to mend or repair, restore what was lost, and equip them for a blessed future. He also completes them. The Greek word *katartizo* means "to mend; to complete; to equip—the process of repairing and restoring what has been damaged, reorienting what has been knocked askew, rearranging, refitting, reequipping as part of an ongoing but inevitable process of making complete or whole once again."[24]

Boaz saw Ruth's integrity even before noticing how beautiful she was. An important lesson if you plan to remarry someday is: find a man who falls in love with your integrity, not your beauty.

In my second book, *Walking with Ruth 5-Day Devotional* (an eBook), I shared,

> During her life, Ruth's trust led them right into the path of redemption. God rewarded her loyalty and faithfulness with a new life and a new future after all of her losses. Boaz became Ruth's kinsman redeemer. This was a privileged position, where a man would take care of relatives who were in danger or in need. Boaz protected and delivered Ruth after the ladies were left penniless and without male protection.
> In chapter 3 of Ruth, she asked Boaz, "Spread the corner of your covering over me, for you are my family redeemer." In the Hebrew, corner means "wings." She was asking to be taken under his wing. She was asking for his coverage of protection, just as Naomi had told her to do. Boaz exemplifies God's provision and protection for us women after divorce. He, too, wants to cover you with His wings and keep you safe during this time. This story is also a beautiful example of God's redemption for all of His beloved children.

Throughout Ruth's story, God was there writing restoration history (His-story). He wasn't the main character in this book, He was merely a quiet participant restoring and redeeming her life.

God stays connected to His people, the ones no one seems to care about, most times working out the details they cannot see, long before they happen. Your suffering won't last, because God has future plans. Trust Him. Wait for Him to reveal that plan, and have courage during the really tough times. He really does have a plan to restore your life and give you your heart's desires, even if that is a loving marriage once again. Do you trust Him enough to keep following His path, staying close to Him without knowing what lies ahead? He accepts you right where you are on this journey, as long as you and He are walking together.

Quiet Patience (Hannah)

I can be patient, even in my current season, but I have a very hard time being quiet. My God-given design is to never shut up. That's probably because I'm easily annoyed. As well as mouthy, I'm easily frustrated when things don't go how I think they should go—a way that is right and fair for all. That's only right—correct? Things should at least be fair! But they aren't always. This is something God has been working on in me since I became a Christian in 1998. At first, the sin I had to be cleansed of was road rage. I traveled from one side of the city of Holland, Michigan, to the other side twice every day for work. It was a trip of fewer than ten miles, but it often took thirty minutes or more one way. Those of you living in big cities understand that frustration.

I was young, drove a five-speed manual transmission car, and just wanted people to move so I could get to work or home. One event that sticks in my mind as a growth experience happened while I was driving home. I was just a few short minutes from home when I went through a yellow, left-hand turn light. I was immediately pulled over by a policeman I must have missed. The officer said I ran a red light. I tried to argue because it wasn't red when I entered the intersection, but he gave me a ticket anyway. He said, "See you in court," when I asked about objecting to this unfair ticket. Frustrated, young, and not knowing what to do, and fearing what a judge would say, I just paid the ticket.

I was a new Christian yearning for this question to be answered: *Why didn't God protect me from getting this ticket I clearly didn't deserve?* Well, because He needed me to learn quiet patience in the face of adversity. I needed to learn when to keep my mouth shut and when to have boldness in speech. (I should not have argued with the police officer that day. Maybe he would have given me more grace instead of a ticket.) I needed to learn that when God holds you up from getting somewhere quickly, He's often protecting you from something down the road you cannot see. He sees and knows more than we give Him credit for, and He allows things to happen to teach us valuable life lessons.

Road rage became road patience after I grew in my faith and understanding about God's protection. What I viewed as a tractor hogging the road and holding me up, He had positioned as a yield sign to keep me from an unknown danger up ahead. In my twenty-plus years as a Christian, I've seen many avoided accidents. Even my divorce, which I felt like was taking forever, slowed me up to plan my future as a single mother. I needed patience while God worked out the final details that needed to happen so I could have a better outcome. I now see how my slow divorce was part of His plan to work things out for good.

I also had to let my marriage go, trusting Him for what He is protecting me from today—repeated, unrepentant infidelity. During visitations, I have to let my children go and trust God is watching over my child(ren), even when I couldn't. I know things go on during visits; there are smear campaigns and things that hurt my child and put him at risk for physical and emotional harm, but there is nothing I can do about it. I've learned to have quiet patience, pray, and allow God's will to be done. I've handed each of my children over to Him, knowing that since God blessed me with them, loaning them to me for a time, I can give them back to Him. I can trust that no matter what, they will be taken care of as their heavenly Father sees fit.

My co-parent is my Husband, who calls me His beloved child. He is still writing His story and my children's stories, and He will work all things out for good, even when I cannot see them. I can trust God even when things seem so uncertain, even when I don't have a relationship with my children. My character always speaks for itself, so I don't have to defend it. I just need to stay silent, unless God asks me to speak, like I do for other women who've experienced exactly what I've experienced. I use my voice for good instead of arguing with those who won't hear me or anything I have to say.

Going Deeper

READ 1 SAMUEL 1 AND 2:1–11. DOES ANYTHING STAND OUT?

WRITE PSALM 37:7.

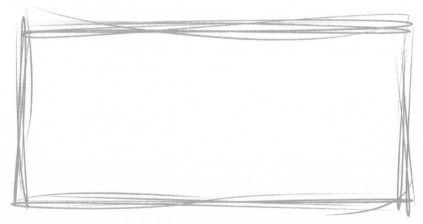

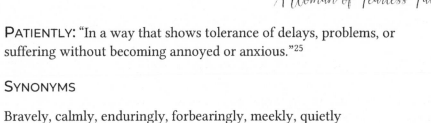

PATIENTLY: "In a way that shows tolerance of delays, problems, or suffering without becoming annoyed or anxious."[25]

SYNONYMS

Bravely, calmly, enduringly, forbearingly, meekly, quietly

WHAT CAUSES ME THE MOST ANXIETY?

AM I ABLE TO ACCEPT GOD'S TIMING OF THINGS?

WHAT CAN I DO TO HELP TO BE STILL WHEN I REALLY WANT TO SPEAK OR ACT, AND IT'S NOT TIME?

WHEN GOD DOES ASK ME TO SPEAK UP, AM I READY TO COMPLY?

Biblically Speaking

Hannah, which means "favor and graciousness," was the mother of the prophet Samuel and wife of Elkanah. Although only mentioned briefly in two short chapters in the Bible, Hannah made a huge statement of faith and trust for provision, especially for the human heart's desires. "Take delight in the Lord, and he will give you the desires of your heart" (Psalm 37:4). She could have been left out of the story completely, as she's just the mother of a prophet, but God saw it necessary to include her in His redemption story.

Hannah was barren, which was considered a curse, while motherhood was a great blessing. Jewish laws at that time allowed a man to divorce his wife if she did not bear a child in the first ten years of marriage. Because of her barrenness, and instead of divorcing her, her husband took a second wife, Peninnah, after that ten-year wait for a child. Hannah was a very passive woman and the favored wife. Peninnah was more aggressive, and she was abusive toward her. Peninnah ridiculed Hannah—the strong mocking the weak—because of her own insecurity over the fact she was an unloved second wife, only in the family to bear children. Instead of trying to defend herself, Hannah just stayed quiet, patiently enduring, taking delight in the Lord and seeking her Defender in prayer. She asked God for her heart's deepest desire, for a child. Being abused by the second wife only increased her pain and struggle over this unfair situation.

"The Lord will fight for you; you need only to be still" (Exodus 14:14). A meek person like Hannah doesn't automatically react or respond because she remains still and allows God to do the defending. But she also knew when to speak up and use her voice (vv. 15–16) in the face of conflict from toxic people. She defended herself against the false accusations of Eli. Instead of going to her earthly husband for comfort and protection, she took her concerns directly to the Lord.

> Being meek does not make you weak. You're not someone who sways with changing circumstances. You don't allow yourself to be used. You're not passive or spineless. Your faith is in the Almighty,

so you know that you are mighty. (Toni Sorenson, *Aligned with Christ*)

Hannah accepted the promise with faith, knowing in time all would be taken care of. She shared her heart with God and sought Him in her barren season. She knew children were coming; she just didn't know when. God didn't condemn her for not being content while she waited patiently for this child—what a relief for people who struggle with being upset with God as they wait for His redemption and restoration!

Hannah's firstborn child Samuel, meaning "asked of God" or "heard of God," was given to her at just the right time—God's time. Other women of the Bible didn't wait so patiently for God to act when they were infertile. Sarah and Rachel took matters in their own hands, causing themselves more grief that could have been avoided. Hannah was a woman of great faith and sang songs of thanksgiving and prophecy of the coming Messiah (1 Samuel 2:6). She dedicated and consecrated her firstborn to the Lord, despite knowing he might end up being her only child.

To wait on God is to live a life of desire towards him, delight in him, dependence on him, and devotedness to him. (Matthew Henry, *The Quest for Meekness and Quietness of Spirit*)

Once she weaned the promised child God had given her, Hannah released him back to God and Eli, the high priest—an easily confused man and a not-so-responsible parent figure himself. Single mothers need to remember this when they have to send their child to visitations with someone they don't trust. God goes with this beloved child, and there is a bigger purpose in all of this. The things the child is experiencing, which can't be avoided, may be part of his or her life story. God will redeem all of it for a purpose. Hannah proved to be strong, resourceful, and independent, even of her own husband. Hannah is an example of what a Christian woman's character should be like. Have a positive attitude even while experiencing difficulties and abuse. Know your value when someone mocks you or tells you you're worthless. Know where to turn for guidance, especially when waiting on the Lord to provide, redeem, and restore.

In Hannah's final prayer, she praised God for assisting the weak in her thanksgiving song. She prayed and thanked the Lord for her struggles and the many blessings that came out of those struggles. God hears and rescues the weak. His lovingkindness is always for them. Her strength came from the Lord. She depended on the Rock of her salvation, and He provided what her heart desired. Through Hannah's story, you see God's heart for your desires. It's not a sin to want something other than what you currently have. He just requests that you bring those desires to Him and wait patiently for Him to provide, without coveting what your neighbor has (there is a difference). And He asks that you be content as much as possible while you wait for Him to deliver on His promises.

Hannah's story was part of God's bigger plan to restore the world—Hisstory. Samuel went on to anoint two kings of Israel, one of them David. God was glorified through both Hannah and Samuel. And He'll be glorified through you, your children (if applicable), and your story as well, in His perfect timing. In the meantime, practice having quiet patience with a faithful heart.

Courage (Esther)

Toward the end of my divorce legal process, I felt that everyone was taking advantage of my weak state and lack of courage to speak up for my children and myself. I was scared. I knew the worst thing that could happen would be to lose custody of my children, especially since he had filed for full custody and asked the court to make me pay him child support. I worried the court would believe his lies and he'd fulfill his threat to take my children from me. I do not like confrontation. I just wanted it to be easy and get my half of the family finances, custody of the kids, and time to get on my feet as a single parent. But that didn't seem to be happening. My lawyer and his lawyer weren't listening to what I needed to survive; they didn't seem to even care. Then, what was said in mediation was not what was on paper. Each time there was a setback, I felt so much fear and anxiety that I wasn't eating or sleeping most days. I didn't trust anyone, not even God at this point. Thankfully, He accepts these feelings from His beloved daughters without repercussions.

My lawyer was telling me not to worry, that my (now ex-) husband would financially take care of us (in a patronizing "Why don't you believe him?" voice), but I knew better. I no longer believed the lies and empty promises that were only an act to impress other people. I had been down this path with this man before. I knew it was all words that would never become actions. I knew I needed to have everything in writing or I'd be experiencing the same things I'd seen in the past. But I didn't have the mindset to face this battle. I wanted to wave the white flag. I felt like the only one on my team to fight for what was right and fair.

Thankfully God "gives strength to the weary and increases the power of the weak" (Isaiah 40:29). In the final days before we were set to go to trial, I had a seed of faith burst open from somewhere deep inside of me. I knew I needed to speak up after going along with what everyone else was telling me I needed to do. I knew I needed to speak up not only for myself and my children (so I could take care of them) but also to show others I could do it without their help. I was ready to face court, knowing I could lose everything and even go to jail for contempt of court, but I trusted God that even if I did, He would take care of things behind the scenes and do things I could not see.

One sleepless night I wrote down everything I would need to financially survive and parent my child after the divorce was final. I came up with a fair and just final decree, considering my circumstances (remember, I like things to be fair). This was my declaration and all I was going to accept in order to sign the divorce papers. The next day, I invited my soon-to-be ex over to discuss my terms one last time. I wasn't willing to accept anything less, and he was just ready for the divorce to be finalized, so he agreed to most everything. I said I would email everything to our lawyers. I knew my lawyer and his lawyer, and I knew he could turn it all against me, forcing the judge to sign the other papers for me. I'd receive whatever he suggested or nothing at all. In faith, I was willing to stand before the judge and explain my situation and tell him how unfairly I felt I was being treated by both lawyers and my husband. I was ready to share that I believed I was fighting this battle for my children. I risked everything to gain what I felt was right and fair. God was by my side and gave me the strength to speak up when I needed to, even while I was shaking in my boots.

We didn't end up going to trial, and everything was finalized within weeks. I don't suggest anyone handle things the way I did, but I also know we often have to take risks for the greater good and to see God's power inside of us and protecting us. Now I see why I needed to have everything I was fighting for written down in the final divorce papers; even though it's in writing, I still have to push to get any follow-through to this day. It was what was in the best interest of everyone and still is today. I am very thankful that God was with me every step of the way, with His strength. And it was the affirmation I needed at the time.

Going Deeper

READ ESTHER 4 AND 2:1–19. DOES ANYTHING STAND OUT?

WRITE HEBREWS 13:6.

COURAGE: "The quality of mind or spirit that enables a person to face difficulty, danger, pain, etc., without fear."[26]

SYNONYMS

Bold, daring, courageous, fearless, unshakable, valiant

DO I HAVE CONFIDENCE AND COURAGE IN THE FACE OF MY TRIALS AND BIGGEST FEARS?

CAN I TRUST GOD'S PROVIDENCE AND PROTECTION, NO MATTER THE OUTCOME?

IS HE ASKING ME TO DO OR SAY SOMETHING WITH GREAT COURAGE?

Biblically Speaking

Esther was a Jewish orphan living in a foreign land because her ancestors were still in captivity for their disobedience to God. After her parent's death, her cousin Mordecai raised her as his own daughter. This ordinary, brave, young lady, with internal and external beauty, went on to become a Persian queen. Why is her story so influential today? Because she teaches valuable lessons that walk women through their faith, with the confidence that no matter what, God is sovereign. He is the supreme authority. Esther listened to wise counsel and submitted to God's plan and purpose with a tender heart, despite her painful upbringing. She took great risks for what was right and fair in her world. She saved many lives through that strength and courage.

Similarly to Hannah, Esther knew when to be still and pray and when to have bravery and faith that God would guide her words and actions for the greater good. At that time, it was against the law, punishable by death, to go uninvited to see the king. Esther was willing to die to save the Jewish people from this pagan king. Through it all, she trusted God and His timing, and relied on Him for strength. She prayed and waited for God's perfect timing to stand up and speak. Through her trust in God's strength, she used her influence to change or *katergazomai* the king's order. The Greek word *katergazomai,* pronounced kat-er-gad'-zom-ahee, means "to perform, accomplish, or achieve something through strength or hard work."[27] Not only did Esther have the courage to accomplish the goal, but God also worked things out and brought the threat of genocide to an end. Every year, in March, Jews still commemorate this deliverance from Haman and the saving of lives with a festival.

> After the fighting had ended, a special feast was held to celebrate this deliverance of the Jews. Called the Feast of Purim, it was then established as a yearly celebration of the blessings received from the Lord during this time. (Jane McBride Choate, *Scriptural Giants: Courageous Queen Esther)*

Esther's story is a lesson in God's sovereignty. It's one of the most important principles of the Christian faith. God created the universe and He has wisdom and oversight of everything in it. He doesn't control us like any human, like King Ahasuerus did—with selfishness and domination in His heart. Instead, God's sovereignty is based on love. It is His permanent nature to serve what He created with His perfect, fatherly love.

Throughout history, the people of this earth didn't trust God to keep His promises for providence or protection. He loved even while giving them consequences, such as staying in the wilderness. Yet all those times, God was still there working out the details, arranging circumstances, and redeeming the stories. Trying to get His people to the promised land, He was writing their story one story at a time.

The Bible proves time and time again that God still loves humans, provides for them, protects them, and gives them power and strength they cannot possess on their own. He gives them tasks and a purpose and then prepares them for that purpose and position. He raises them up to that position to do the job only they can do, as he did with Esther, whose uncle told her, "If you remain silent at this time, relief and deliverance for the Jews will arise from another place, but you and your father's family will perish. And who knows but that you have come to your royal position for such a time as this?" (Esther 4:14).

These five women of fearless faith knew the greatness of God and had the boldness of speech and took action at the exact moment they were needed. This didn't end in the first couple of centuries. And even though you may struggle with same mistrust, God still loves, provides, and protects until the end of time and space. You are created for such a time as this! Stand up tall and be courageous, sister! He is with you and goes before you, preparing the way.

Week 5
My Heart and Mind Renewed in Christ

THE PEACE OF GOD, WHICH
TRANSCENDS ALL UNDERSTANDING,
WILL GUARD YOUR HEARTS AND YOUR
MINDS IN CHRIST JESUS.
—PHILIPPIANS 4:7

Accepted, Not Rejected

One Christmas, while I was married, my mother-in-law bought me a knockoff Vera Wang, paisley, fabric purse with a matching compact wallet. That year those purses were all the rage, and many women were carrying them on their shoulders. Personally, I don't wear or carry anything that looks like curtains. If she had asked me what I liked and spent a little time getting to know me, she would have known that was never something I'd carry around. The compact wallet wasn't even big enough for all the things I carry in my wallet; however, I thanked her kindly for the gift, took it home, and placed it in back of the closet with all the other things I didn't know what to do with (many of the things she had given me through the years that were not to my taste). I don't mean to sound mean or bitter, but her lack of consideration for what I would want was an ongoing problem that was never resolved, even after I tried to bring it to her attention. No apologies were given, only blame, as always. I truly wanted to be loved and accepted by her, but that never happened.

One day I found a purpose for that paisley purse. I needed to replace the sewing basket my grandmother-in-law gave me, after I had told her I needed one. It was literally smashed and in pieces after my children sat on it one too many times. So I took everything out of the basket and put all my sewing supplies into my new paisley sewing bag. The little pockets on the inside of the purse are perfect for jars of odd buttons, pins, and spools of thread. It became such a useful sewing bag! A couple of months later, my mother-in-law found out I wasn't using the bag as a purse, and I heard from another family member that she was very upset. My only guess is she felt rejected by me for rejecting her gift. She never said a word to me about her feelings. If she had, I would have said I didn't reject it, I valued the bag for what I wanted to use it for. I've made this rejected purse very useful—I still have it to this day.

As someone who has had her gifts rejected, and been rejected personally, I know how it feels to be the giver of the paisley knockoff purse. I know these purses were very popular at one time; maybe they still are. That tells me I might be one of the few who rejected these popular purses. My individual rejection means nothing when the company looks at the number of purchases of their product and how much their revenue is. Their sales establish their worth, not one woman in the United States who cares more about a natural look than bold colors and patterns. Thinking about the paisley purse reminds me of myself in many ways. I often wished my family would have woken up one day to see my value, to see I was worthy of a purpose and not worthless. I'm not sure why many people throughout my life didn't see me as useful or important.

My critical family members are the type to make anyone and everyone the butt of their jokes, especially those who look different, like I did. Being the only natural blond-haired and blue-eyed girl, I was always the dumb blonde. If I only had a dollar for every blonde joke I was told. My parents divorced when I was seven, which left me without a father in my life, and my mother was too busy to be an active parent in my life. Then I was bullied by my older brother, who was supposed to take care of me. I was alone a lot and often felt rejected. But "though my father and mother forsake me, the Lord will receive me" (Psalm 27:10). Just because my family and former husband didn't appreciate what I brought to the table or accept me for who I am or was created to be, it doesn't mean I'm unacceptable or rejected. I may have that wound, but my wounds don't define me. As I stand on faith and rebuild my life after divorce, finding healing from all of those wounds, I choose to focus on good things and the acceptance I have in Christ.

"Finally, brothers and sisters, whatever is true, whatever is noble, whatever is right, whatever is pure, whatever is lovely, whatever is admirable—if anything is excellent or praiseworthy—think about such things" (Philippians 4:8). I believe my deep emotional wounds caused me to live in a place of self-protection, needing to be healed before I was healthy enough to find, accept, and receive love in a healthy way. Most people who suffer from rejection wounds will undervalue themselves while allowing all later relationships to do the same. I had done that for way too long, so now I find it imperative to make sure I am feeling accepted by my Creator before moving forward.

Knowing and believing we are accepted, not rejected, is one of the cornerstones of our emotional and spiritual healing. Knowing we have a purpose, even if others don't see it, helps us to feel loved in a world full of unloving, unkind people.

Going Deeper

READ 1 PETER 2:4–10 AND 1 TIMOTHY 4. DOES ANYTHING STAND OUT?

WRITE 1 TIMOTHY 4:4.

ACCEPTANCE: "Regarded favorably: given approval or acceptance; being received with approval or pleasure."[28]

SYNONYMS

Acknowledged, approved, chosen, established, favorable, recognized

DO I FEEL ACCEPTED BY GOD?

IF EVERYTHING GOD CREATED IS GOOD, DOESN'T THAT MEAN I AM GOOD AND ACCEPTABLE TO HIM TOO?

DO I LET THE FACT THAT I AM NOT REJECTED BY GOD, THROUGH FAITH, HELP ME TO HEAL MY WOUNDS OF REJECTION?

Biblically Speaking

If you've experienced a lot of rejection in your life, you could be used to wearing a mask without even knowing why. Rejection is very much part of the human experience; even God in the flesh knew rejection. It's one of the biggest struggles many humans face. Even without knowing it, your rejection wound could lead to isolation, disappointment, anger, sadness, and depression. You may feel the need to remain isolated to protect yourself from further hurt, or you might become very anxious around new people, while also feeling lonely and needing connection in your life. Rejection wounds become embedded in your memory, altering the way you see yourself and the way you relate to other people, even altering the way you relate to God. Sometimes there are wounds deeply rooted in your heart and soul that cause you to overprotect, so deep you cannot see them. What you may believe to be merely perfectionism or people pleasing is really your rejection wound trying to heal itself.

To reject means "to throw back, resist, refuse, or despise something or someone." When you don't like something, you reject it. Often, those with the biggest rejection wounds reject people more often than others. This is very normal. They reject others because they've never learned or experienced acceptance. Divorce is the ultimate form of rejection of a spouse—many people leave before a spouse leaves them. In Bible times, a husband would write up a bill of divorce for the wife of his youth to reject her from the home and his life, which was very harsh at that time and the reason for the statement: "The man who hates and divorces his wife," says the Lord, the God of Israel, "does violence to the one he should protect" (Malachi 2:16). The women during that time had no ability to provide for themselves after divorce beyond family charity or prostitution. They didn't have the rights or resources we have today to survive. God hates divorce because of its violence and hatred toward women, not because He wants to punished divorced women.

God is not rejecting you; He accepts you. You need acceptance to heal the rejection wound.

> Our giant of rejection is not going to fall until we admit that we desperately need acceptance. The good news is that in Christ, we have everything we long for. Everything we need. We are not working to gain his acceptance. We already have it. We live from acceptance, not for the acceptance of others. (Louie Giglio, *Goliath Must Fall*)

God knows rejection because humans have rejected Him since the garden. Jesus was rejected on earth yet still is the cornerstone of redemption. He is the connection point, the most important piece of building material you need when regaining your life after divorce. God never rejects His beloved (sons and) daughters. Actually, He's willing to purchase you back and redeem your life. He really wants you to feel His acceptance and His love for you. You are His masterpiece.

JESUS IS THE CORNERSTONE

"The stone the builders rejected has become the cornerstone" (Psalm 118:22). The Bible references construction materials often because the people of that time were familiar with building their own homes. As you studied in week one, faith is built upon a solid foundation. That solid foundation is Jesus. He is the rejected cornerstone. In Bible times, the first stone set in any construction of a building was the cornerstone. Referred to as the foundation stone, it was picked out of the pile of "best of the best" stones—only a perfect stone would do to hold such an important position in the building. Any stone that wasn't perfect was rejected for this sacred position.

Perfect Jesus redeemed you, taking the ultimate rejection. He was rejected by His brothers (John 7:5), rejected by Jewish leaders (Luke 4:24), and even physically rejected by God for three days after death (Mark 15:34). But the cross brought you reconciliation and redemption with God. After being rejected by humans, Jesus still reached out His loving hand to wipe away your rejection. Jesus took God's wrath on the cross. He was the innocent who took the wrath for the guilty—all humans. He was rejected and still placed in the highest honor as the cornerstone. Faith is your response; you are given the same high honor. You are His beloved, His child, and His bride.

> The only thing that will help us move past the giant of rejection is to immerse ourselves in the acceptance of Christ. (Louie Giglio, *Goliath Must Fall*)

When you're feeling rejected, guard and renew your mind with what the cornerstone, the rejected Savior did for you on the cross. This is the solid foundation on which your new, emotionally healthy life needs to be rebuilt—your repaired faith.

> Consequently, you are no longer foreigners and strangers, but fellow citizens with God's people and also members of his household, built on the foundation of the apostles and prophets, with Christ Jesus himself as the chief cornerstone. In him the whole building is joined together and rises to become a holy temple in the Lord. And in him you too are being built together to become a dwelling in which God lives by his Spirit. (Ephesians 2:19–22)

As a believer, you are fully armed with the Holy Spirit to view yourself through God's eyes and believe yourself loved and accepted. You have all you need to fight the temptation of the enemy to believe otherwise.

My Heart Surrender

At some point in my marriage, I realized I had become a passive, timid wife with a bit of passive-aggression on the side. As the end drew near, I felt as though I was manipulated and expected to remain in that position, which made me very angry. In my mind, I believed that being a wife and mother was my one and only purpose in life. I wasn't Jen, the educated woman with God-given gifts and life goals of her own. No, my only reason for being alive was to be a "good little wifey" who did what she was told and raised quiet, respectful children.

I'm not bitter about that time I spent at home raising or homeschooling my children. I have fond memories and am thankful for the experiences of doing Girl Scouts, going on field trips, helping in classrooms when my kids were in school, and keeping score at their sporting events. But I'm also sad the submission and surrendering of myself to being a mother and wife for life was motivated by obligation to do so. Any complaint about not getting any time away for myself to refuel or to do something beyond raising children or taking care of the house was met with objections—we never had the money for that—and disapproval.

After my divorce, I learned I have worth beyond my home and family. I realized I was actually in bondage, surrendered to humans instead of my Maker. I've learned I was created for so much more than just the season of motherhood. Divorce changed my perspective and gave me hope. I was created for so much more than this. My heart has also been changed. My motivation for doing things is not because I have to or because I might get in trouble. I surrender to authority because I wholeheartedly want to. No longer am I self-centered or motivated by self-righteousness to perform for anyone. Instead, I feel led by a need to fulfill a purpose while being led by the Holy Spirit to bring the same hope to other women who are trapped in the same sort of bondage I was in. My mission is to do God's work, and my work is saving many lives (Genesis 50:20). Since daily walking in my purpose, I feel like Moses, walking with women out of their oppression, with no real knowledge about how we'll get to the promised land. The Lord says to walk and He guides the way. I cannot do this on my own. I often feel like I'm not equipped to do this task or someone else is better equipped than me. But I just keep asking for my daily assignment, while completing the task before me. This year it has been to complete this book.

When we are successful in love, or financially, we think we don't need God. Don't we all love that security system that tells us we've got this all under control? Then God allows the rug to be pulled out from under us, so to speak, and we're left at the end of ourselves. Reaching dead ends or feeling like we've hit rock bottom can be the best places for us to learn to trust God instead of our own ingenuity or another human—even the one who vowed to love, honor, and cherish until death. Divorce was that rock bottom for me. It taught me to lean on God, be yoked to Him, and allow Him to lead. God allows us free will so when we get to that dead-end place, where He is all that's left, we're willing to wave the white flag and surrender to Him. The legal process got me to that point. I had no one else to turn to. And since my divorce, He has been my everything and the Rock under me. I now know I can surrender myself to Him because He is a trustworthy and loving Husband.

After giving up my will and completely surrendering my heart, I gained forgiveness, peace, and joy. But I had to let go of what I thought my life was supposed to look like in order to allow God to use me—all of me, all the pieces and insecurities I had always hidden from others. There is no longer a need to find acceptance because I'm already accepted, being both a hot mess and adored. And because I'm accepted, I carry no shame. What others think or say about me doesn't matter. I am always accepted. Now, the only place I ever want to be is inside God's will, following His path. I may get off course for a time, but I know He's always there waiting for me right where I left off. And when troubles and trials come, because they always do, I know I'm safely protected and held close under His wing.

Going Deeper

READ JAMES 4. DOES ANYTHING STAND OUT?

WRITE JAMES 4:7.

SUBMIT: "Accept or yield to a superior force or to the authority or will of another person; subject to a particular process, treatment, or condition."[29]

SYNONYMS

Abide, agree, comply, relinquish, succumb, surrender

WHAT'S MY HEART SURRENDER?

DO I YIELD TO GOD'S LEADING AND SURRENDER TO HIS WILL?

DO I DO SO OUT OF OBLIGATION, TO IMPRESS OTHERS, OR BECAUSE THAT'S MY HEART'S DESIRE?

Biblically Speaking

Many women don't like the word "submit," especially those who were submissive during their marriage to appease a husband who in turn abused them. After divorce, the word still seems harsh because it's thought that to submit is to give up all your rights as a woman or a human being. You may have wanted to rebel against authority in order to prove no one can bring you down to that low point ever again. But God's idea of surrendering and submitting to Him is not the world's or man's idea of submission. He's not like any human. He loves you better than any human will. He only and always wants what is best for you and your life.

When you get up and go to work or an appointment, you submit to that obligation or authority. When you follow the speed limit, wear your seatbelt (or a mask), and stop texting while driving, you do so because it's mandatory. And there are punishments if you get caught not doing these things. Not obeying the laws of the land could cause you more pain and heartache through tickets, accidents, or worse. When you love your job and what you do, you get up, go, and do because you truly want to go to work and do what you're obligated to do. You discipline your children or fur babies because you know it needs to be done, not because you want to. It's what is for the best because you love them and don't want them harmed. There is greater good to do hard things for. That's the heart difference between doing something because you have to and doing something because you want to.

> Every day, we have to ask God for our assignment, we must not assume we understand His plan but rather surrender to His will daily. (E'yen A. Gardner, *Humbly Submitting to Change*)

To surrender is to give up, yield, or submit. Surrender is letting go of what you thought life should look like to embrace what God has planned—His mission and purpose for your life. Give up control over what happens next, your need to be in charge, your need to have all the answers and every detail planned out. Give up control over your divorce and release anything or anyone you're holding too tightly to here on earth. Walk with God into the unknown future—often a future of uncertainty—trusting Him to guide, provide, and protect you from further harm. Jesus asks if you are willing to follow Him, giving up whatever He asks you to give up or release in order to follow Him and His will. Jesus needed the disciples' complete surrender. They had to walk away from money, possessions, and even family. Jesus needs you to surrender in order to continue the work of the Holy Spirit in your life. In return, He offers you so much more than earthly possessions. "Whoever does the will of my Father in heaven is my brother and sister and mother" (Matthew 12:50).

God is the only One who completely understands your every feeling, all you've been through and all that has happened to you. Not only does He lead you to His will, but His spirit also keeps doing the work and healing needed in you to walk in your purpose. Growth is an ongoing process. It happens moment by moment as you seek what He has for you next.

> One does not surrender a life in an instant. That which is lifelong can only be surrendered in a lifetime. Nor is surrender to the will of God (per se) adequate to fullness of power in Christ. Maturity is the accomplishment of years, and I can only surrender to the will of God as I know what that will is. (Elisabeth Elliot, *Shadow of the Almighty: The Life and Testament of Jim Elliot*)

Ask God to use you to fulfill His purpose for your life while protecting you from the enemy's attack. The Father will prepare you as you wait for the vision and His plan becomes clearer and clearer. Seek out godly input and wise counsel to gain more wisdom.

> I will instruct you and teach you in the way you should go; I will counsel you [who are willing to learn] with My eye upon you. Do not be like the horse or like the mule which have no understanding, Whose trappings include bridle and rein to hold them in check, Otherwise they will not come near to you. (Psalm 32:8–9 AMP)

My Authentic Self

When I meet people who seem to be free to be spunky, loud, funny, honest, and genuinely themselves, unafraid of anyone's criticism, I think to myself, *I wish I could be more like them.* I love flamboyant and gutsy people. I seem to be drawn to them. My friend Erin is one of those people who can dye her hair all the colors of the rainbow, which looks great on her, and not be worried about what anyone else thinks. I think her personality is such that she enjoys her colored hair and is not worried about anyone's negative reaction. Why can't I be bolder and embrace bright-colored hair? What stops me? Besides my middle age, I've never felt so free to do anything I want to make myself physically stand out. I often didn't feel free to be who I wanted to be. Someone always had an opinion, and those opinions held more weight than my own for much of my life until I learned to be more authentic. Why did I let so many people control who I was?

In the past, when I met a woman who was assertive, direct, firm in her convictions, and unapologetic in her boundaries, I thought she was mean or didn't like me at first. But once I got to know her and saw she had a really kind heart, I wanted to be just like them. Again, I always found it interesting that Erin was free to her own way of thinking and acting, yet I felt forced to be passive, quiet, and not have any convictions of my own. Subconsciously reminding myself of all the harsh or negative things people had said about me stopped me in my tracks. I'd shrink back into my turtle shell where everything was safe and pretend to be a quiet, nice, passive Christian woman again—a woman who never stood up for herself because she didn't want to upset anyone. I was a card-carrying member of the people pleasers club. I needed to stop doing anything if it made my family or close friends unhappy and do as they wished instead.

That all changed after my divorce. I wanted to find myself, find what I liked, what I needed, and who I was created to be. So in 2016, I spent the entire year marinating on one word, "authentic." The "one word" idea is a common replacement in Christian circles for setting New Year's resolutions. Instead of making a list of things to change to make life better, a person picks one word and sees how life could be changed by that one word. I called 2016 my year of authenticity. It took me the entire year to decide I wasn't going to allow others to define my actions or my true self any longer. I learned I was allowed to express myself freely, even if someone else didn't like it.

Through my openness, truthfulness, and authenticity, I've been able to open up my life so others can see the destruction called divorce. I've allowed my story to be hope for others who are fighting the storms I have come through. In the process, God has been transforming my life and redeeming my story. My year of authenticity also allowed me to become a better version of myself. No more people pleasing or conceding to the wishes of others. I became freer to have my quirks (that make me *me*), feelings, wants, and a purpose for my life other than taking care of others.

Showing others my imperfect and messy life hasn't been easy. As God has elevated my mission for more of the world to see, I've faced even more resistance and opposition. People have tried to shame me and blame me, always trying to detour me from God's plan. But through my healing, I've released the shame. Shame could have kept me trapped in bondage or in my healing, telling me to keep everything a secret, but now that I've shared my struggles, shame has lost its grip on me. Jesus has washed all my problems, sin, and the divorce white as snow. Now, when someone tries to get me to believe I should be silenced, ashamed, or guilty, I remind myself it only bothers me if I believe it to be true about myself. I can share the truth about my life, even all the embarrassing and sinful things, because I am forgiven. My past has no hold on me because I've brought it all out of the dark into the light, where God can use it for good. Those parts of my life and how I live my life today are my authentic self. This is how God designed me, so I won't be anything else than who I was created to be.

Going Deeper

READ 2 CORINTHIANS 4 AND EPHESIANS 4:17–32. DOES ANYTHING STAND OUT?

WRITE EPHESIANS 4:25.

TRUTHFUL: "Telling or expressing the truth; honest; characterized by accuracy or realism; true to life."[30]

SYNONYMS

Accurate, authentic, candid, genuine, sincere, Veritable,

AM I ABLE TO BE MY TRUE AUTHENTIC, GENUINE SELF?

WHAT OR WHO HOLDS ME BACK FROM LIVING OUT MY AUTHENTIC SELF?

DO I HIDE THE TRUTH ABOUT MYSELF BECAUSE I FEEL SILENCED, ASHAMED, OR GUILTY?

AS I READ 2 CORINTHIANS 4 AND EPHESIANS 4, IS THAT WHAT I'M WORKING ON AFTER MY DIVORCE?

Biblically Speaking

In order to regain yourself after divorce, you must put away your former life to embrace the future. Maybe for you, the former consisted of masks, falsehoods, and untruths about yourself in order to fit into the mold someone else created: be the best wife or the perfect mother. You may have walked on eggshells around your husband—silent submission—and felt as though you've lost yourself in the process of making everyone else happy. Women are expected to have it altogether. Christians are expected to be strong and courageous yet meek and quiet. Other people don't want to see your pain or struggles because Christians are supposed to be constantly filled with the joy of the Lord, never with any unhappiness, grief, or sorrow. But the fact is that real life is a struggle. It's hard to be strong and keep it all inside when your world is falling apart and things aren't going your way. Bad things happen to good people every single day. And most everyone on earth has experienced something traumatic in his or her life, at one point or another. You are free to struggle.

Authenticity is accepting what has happened, what you did wrong or right, accepting the struggle and that you haven't yet arrived at perfection because you never will. It's allowing yourself to feel whatever feelings you are feeling when you're feeling them. Being authentic means you're a work in progress, trying to be your best self every day without holding anything back. All the Lord asks is that you be truthful about everything, especially about who He created you to be.

> Authenticity is the daily practice of letting go of who we think we're supposed to be and embracing who we are. (Brené Brown, *The Gifts of Imperfection: Let Go of Who You Think You're Supposed to Be and Embrace Who You Are*)

All humans are fallible. You have imperfections because everyone has imperfections and no one is perfect. Humans can learn from their mistakes or hide them away and pretend they don't exist. Instead of hiding your imperfections behind makeup or masks of perfectionism, you can be authentic. You just have to open yourself up to the entire truth. The first step is to be honest with yourself. The more honest you are with yourself, the more you'll be able to accept the truth about who you really are. That truth will set you free—free to be your authentic self, free from trying to please others, and free from any heaviness or shame you may carry.

Your true inner self is who God created you to be, flaws and all. He created you and allowed you to make those mistakes so you could live more fully in what He has planned for you. God loves those inner parts because He created them, and everything God created is accepted, not rejected, as you learned earlier this week (in 1 Timothy 4:4). But you must start with accepting yourself.

Progress, not perfection, is the goal when learning to be authentic. Acceptance, self-love, and vulnerability are the keys to unlocking the door to who you really are and who you were created to be. Your true self is already known and accepted, so now just continue in the process, accepting the transformation each and every day, knowing you will never arrive at perfect. You're just going to have to accept your authentic self in the journey to get there.

> To be authentic, we must cultivate the courage to be imperfect— and vulnerable. We have to believe that we are fundamentally worthy of love and acceptance, just as we are. (Brené Brown)

I Am Bittersweet

I love my children very much. As I've shared, they have been my entire world for most of their lives. Looking back and evaluating my parenting skills, I wasn't perfect, but I did the very best I could do as a mother. I taught them be hardworking, respectful, and kind people to the rest of the world. I often tell my youngest son, since he is the only one still under the age of eighteen, that I will be proud of him even if he's a bus driver, garbage man, or mechanic—as long as he is a kind human being. It's not the job that makes a person important; it is the character behind the person. That's something to be most proud of and the only thing you take with you when you leave this earth.

At the same time, I am bitter that one of the consequences of a too-long, toxic marriage has been the poor and often disrespectful way my children treat me. They repeatedly witnessed me being dishonored and disrespected as a human being, and I allowed it. I didn't assert boundaries and I didn't leave after repeated infidelity. I believe they were taught how I, as their mother, a fellow human being, deserved to be treated. In their minds, I probably never earned their respect because I didn't respect myself enough to walk away when I was disrespected. I didn't have boundaries and lived with a lot of resentment for my lack of them. If I had done a better job of leading by example, I would not have been so foolish, knowing my children were being taught how to treat their mother by an abusive father. "A foolish son is a grief and anguish to his father. And bitterness to her who gave birth to him" (Proverbs 17:25 AMP).

The Bible talks about getting rid of all bitterness (Ephesians 4:31) and not allowing it to take root in our hearts because it can lead us down the wrong paths, leading to sin. But the books of Proverbs and Ruth talk about how women and mothers can be brought to bitterness by the actions of others or their life's circumstances. Bitterness is not all bad all the time. Sometimes women can feel bitterness and learn how to deal with it authentically rather than hide it away.

The definition of "bitter" in the *Oxford English Living Dictionaries* is "feeling or showing anger, hurt, or resentment because of bad experiences or a sense of unjust treatment; painful or unpleasant to accept or contemplate."[31] At times, those are my genuine feelings. I feel like I was and am still being treated unjustly. I'm not angry or holding any resentment but I'm hurt. Who wouldn't be? It is honestly painful to be accused of things I didn't do or say. And no matter what I do, it's just not good enough or done the right way. I've talked to many divorced women who feel this very same way. So many divorced women are estranged from their children or blamed for the divorce, when it wasn't their fault.

I've had to give myself permission to feel all the hard feelings to live my authentic life. God can handle them and help me through the pain. When we deny hard feelings and personal afflictions, they don't go away, they're just hidden, waiting to come out at a later time. They come up again in ways and at times when we least expect them to. But "though you (God) have made me see troubles, many and bitter, you will restore my life again; from the depths of the earth you will again bring me up" (Psalm 71:20). My life is messy and full of hurt. And I can feel hurt while still being hopeful for God's restoration of my life and any broken relationships. I can be bittersweet—a mixture of knowing pain while feeling joy and hopeful. I know even my hard feelings have a purpose. They show me where I need to do repair work and where to apply God's healing.

Over time I've worked through the forgiveness process, accepting where I may have contributed. I've opened up my heart to allow space for healing in those relationships, even if the other people aren't ready. I have to make myself ready, even if it never happens, because my heart healing is for me, not anyone else. This allows the sweetness of life to guide my heart down the right paths instead of the path to anger and sin. I don't want to deny any of the bitter part of my story, just as Naomi didn't with Ruth. I don't want to pretend it's not part of me. My bitterness made me stronger, and the sweetness filled me with more compassion for the rest of the imperfect, bitter mothers in this world. It forced me to push through and be courageous as I faced each obstacle during and after my divorce. I push forward knowing that what is broken will be restored and made beautiful one day.

Going Deeper

READ RUTH 1 AND ECCLESIASTES 3. DOES ANYTHING STAND OUT?

WRITE ISAIAH 30:20–21.

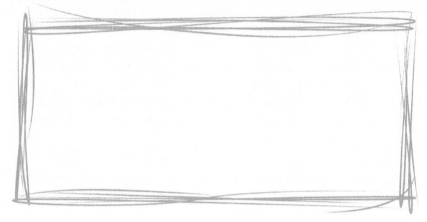

AFFLICTION: "The state of being afflicted; a state of pain, distress, or grief; the cause of continued pain of body or mind, as sickness, losses, calamity, adversity, persecution."[32]

SYNONYMS

Adversity, anguish, distress, grief, hardship, suffering

IN WHAT WAYS AM I BITTER ABOUT A BAD EXPERIENCE OR A TIME OF UNJUST TREATMENT?

HAVE I CLEARED A PLACE FOR HEALING IN MY HEART SO AS TO
WELCOME THE FUTURE INSTEAD OF LIVING IN THE PAST?

Biblically Speaking

According to Ecclesiastes 3 "there is a time for everything, and a season for every activity under the heavens. A time to weep and a time to laugh, a time to mourn and a time to dance." For many, the seasons of hardship are longer, sometimes lifelong, because life as a Christian has no promises of days filled with rainbows and sunshine. People of faith struggle and face many trials, while learning to endure and hold onto hope. "Each heart knows its own bitterness, and no one else can share its joy" (Proverbs 14:10). When you search your heart, you will find your own struggles. No one besides God can know or understand your deepest feelings and emotions unless you share them. Even the most sympathetic human cannot fully comprehend the distress of your heart and the anguish of your mind that needs to be tended to. It is only God who knows exactly what you need to heal your deepest heart wounds. "For who knows a person's thoughts except their own spirit within them? In the same way no one knows the thoughts of God except the Spirit of God" (1 Corinthians 2:11).

Bitterness often arises from external troubles, losses, disappointments, and diseases of the mind or body. It is a temporary feeling, even if it lasts months or years. Having feelings and emotions is part of the human experience given to you by God so that you may relate to Jesus's human experience, so your heart may be softened during its own season of mourning.

Each woman is on her own path, full of hard things and struggles. There is no other friend who can relate so well with your current condition than the

One who suffered much here on earth. He will wipe away every tear (Revelation 21:4). He will bind every wound (Psalm 147:3) and make all things new (Isaiah 43:18). He will work everything out according to His good plans (Romans 8:28). Those are His promises. He keeps His promises (Joshua 21:45).

BITTER NAOMI – Naomi wanted to be known as "Mara" because she thought God had dealt with her harshly or bitterly. "Mara" or "Marah" means "greatly distressed, chafed, discontented, and heavy." Naomi was bitter after losing her husband and her two sons. She lost their financial provision. She felt she had been afflicted with pain and was suffering without having sinned or being deserving of such afflictions. It wasn't fair. God allowed her season of mourning and still rewarded her with restoration of her family. She didn't have to clean herself up for God. She was accepted just the way she was, in the season she was in, because there is a time for goodness too.

BITTER JOB – Job was bitter. He had everything he valued taken away from him for no good reason. He had followed the Law to the letter. That must have felt like injustice. He complained and argued with his friends and God about his troubles for thirty-four-plus chapters in the book of Job. "I will not keep silent; I will speak out in the anguish of my spirit, I will complain in the bitterness of my soul" (Job 7:11). He was in a season of mourning and hurt, giving that pain to God and looking for understanding for why it had happened. Job did not sin in his anger or bitterness; instead, he asked God to restore His life after the season of bitterness.

BITTERSWEET FAITH

Life is often bittersweet with two opposing forces of good and evil, life and death, coming at you every single day, and it's often consuming. It's sweet with a bitter aftertaste. Being emotionally bittersweet is having a mixture of opposing feelings at the same time—a mixture of love and hate or joy and sorrow. You could be dealing with affliction or adversity while feeling growth, healing, and hope for the future. You can have contradictory feelings and still be within God's will and righteousness. Because there is a season for everything, there is a season for the bittersweet.

Bittersweet is the practice of believing that we really do need both the bitter and the sweet, and that a life of nothing but sweetness rots both your teeth and your soul. Bitter is what makes us strong, what forces us to push through, what helps us earn the lines on our faces and the calluses on our hands. Sweet is nice enough, but bittersweet is beautiful, nuanced, full of depth and complexity. Bittersweet is courageous, gutsy, earthy. (Shauna Niequist, *Bittersweet: Thoughts on Change, Grace, and Learning the Hard Way*)

The foundation of your Christian faith is also bittersweet. Jesus's rejection and painful death on the cross, along with the empty tomb and resurrection, are bittersweet. You must embrace the bitter in order to know the sweet. It's like eating a box of dark chocolate every day of the year; it's experiencing the pain and sadness in this world while holding onto the joy that comes to you each morning. After Good Friday's death on the cross comes new life on Sunday. After the dark of night is the light of the sun. After winter is spring—full of hope, growth, and new life.

God doesn't want your heart hardened by unhealed and unresolved issues, but He fully accepts you in each and every season. He sees every tear of grief and mourning and He counts each one (Psalm 56:8). He wants you to pour your broken, burdened heart and all that injustice on Him so He can turn it into sweet joy. Jesus is gentle and humble at heart, ready and willing to guide your heart to healing. "Therefore we do not lose heart. Though outwardly we are wasting away, yet inwardly we are being renewed day by day" (2 Corinthians 4:16).

I Am Enough (Not Too Much!)

Every single time my ex-husband was caught with another woman, everything I ever did or didn't do became the reason for his infidelity. I was either not enough or too much, and sometimes both at the very same time. I was too sensitive, too intense, too compassionate, and too obsessive of him and what he did. Add to that I had too high expectations (according to him), which led him to think he needed to find love and acceptance elsewhere. After the fourth time of finding out about an inappropriate relationship, I told him I wanted to get off that emotional roller coaster. In his mind this was me rejecting him, but he didn't see how many times his words and actions had rejected me over and over again.

Unhealed childhood rejection wounds cause some men to reject the people who love them the most in adulthood—gotta get you before you get them. My deepest rejection wounds have often caused my rejection of myself as well as my rejection of others. I'm often tired of feeling rejected, when all I want to feel is accepted. This causes my inner dialogue to tell me that in order to remain safe from further rejection, I need to pull back and become more introverted and isolated. As a natural introvert, I have to fight my natural tendency to escape and hide under a rock when there is any sort of conflict.

While writing this chapter, I wanted to give up on completing the whole assignment God asked of me. I felt as though I might be rejected for my many writing mistakes, for my lack of complete knowledge of the Bible, and for all the sins I've done in my life—the shame of my imperfect past. I wondered if my work would be accepted, and I doubted it was any good. Even on days of doubt and self-loathing, I have to keep renewing my mind and directing my heart toward what God is having me do. This is where He has me, even if it feels uncomfortable and I feel ill-prepared. I have to remind myself that even if only one person benefits from this book, it was worth the time and effort I put into it. And if this work is enough for God and the kingdom of heaven, then it's enough. Period. I am enough. Never too much. My rewards are in heaven, not on this earth, where rejection is inevitable.

My heart and mind are acceptable to God as long as I'm being renewed and led by the Spirit. It doesn't matter what anyone else on earth thinks or feels about me, not even my own family (who will probably reject me even more for writing this book). Rejection can only hurt me if I believe I'm unacceptable to God. All that matters is what my Abba Daddy knows and judges through Jesus. I'm accepted and not rejected, and He will never leave me or forsake me.

I do His will and continue this work because I'm enough for Him and never too much! I'm perfectly designed in His eyes. I need to remember who I am in Him and not who I am to other people. This is what keeps me going, writing, and fulfilling my purpose.

Going Deeper

READ EPHESIANS 4:21–25. DOES ANYTHING STAND OUT?

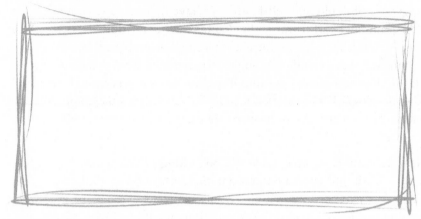

WRITE 2 CORINTHIANS 4:16.

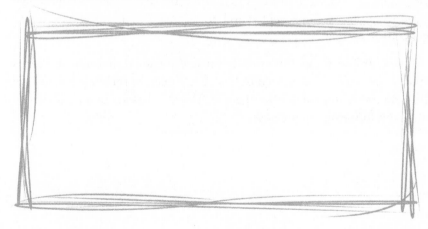

RENEW: "To restore to freshness, vigor, or perfection; to make new spiritually, to restore to existence, to make extensive changes in, to do again, to begin again."[33]

In theology, "to make new; to renovate; to transform; to change from natural enmity to the love of God and His law; to implant holy affections in the heart."[1]

SYNONYMS

Begin again, reaffirm, reawaken, reestablish, restate, revive

DO I REMIND MYSELF I AM ENOUGH (AND NOT TOO MUCH)?

AM I ALLOWING THE WORLD TO TELL ME WHO I AM AND WHO I SHOULD BE?

IN WHAT WAYS DO I FEEL I DON'T MEASURE UP?

How am I renewing my mind to see myself through God's eyes and His purpose for my life, even if I don't yet know what that is?

Biblically Speaking

The devil wants to detour you from thinking, knowing, and believing who you are in Christ—accepted, not rejected. First, his evil forces try to change your mind, then they change your heart to believe you're not enough or you haven't done enough to earn God's love. Then they tell you you're too much for other people, trying to drown your purpose with feelings of doubt and lack of worth. As you start to believe these lies, you forget where to find your hope. But "do not conform to the pattern of this world, but be transformed by the renewing of your mind. Then you will be able to test and approve what God's will is—his good, pleasing and perfect will" (Romans 12:2). In the world you'll face opposition, planted there by your greatest adversary. As your mind wanders away, don't focus on your circumstances or you'll be exhausted on the journey. You have to keep reminding yourself where your focus needs to be. It's an ongoing process. Jesus is your cornerstone. He holds you up during times of struggle and doubt. He says, "Lean on Me and I will give you strength to keep going, growing, and running the race."

The world says titles matter. "Married," "separated," or "divorced" all have different meanings, statuses, and purposes. Young, old, rich, and poor—people look for ways to put people into categories of importance. Many humans have their own rating system of what makes people enough, praiseworthy even, while others are judged as too much and disrespected. The garbage man—is he not enough, not worthy of anything better? The loud singer at church or the crying toddler at the store—are they too much? God doesn't measure people the way humans do. He looks at their heart.

"The Lord doesn't see things the way you see them. People judge by outward appearance, but the Lord looks at the heart" (Samuel 16:7). This is why it's so important to renew your mind. Your heart believes what the mind tells it. The heart needs guidance. It can be easy to say, "I am the daughter of a King, beloved, and a masterpiece," but do you really believe it, deep down in your heart? Renewing your mind is an act of faith, believing the Word of God and His view of you and your purpose. It's being in agreement with God's will. He changes you from the inside out, changing the heart and the mind first.

Don't dilute yourself to make others see you as enough or not too much. If your being small makes someone feel better or like you, you're devaluing yourself. Sister, say it out loud with me: "I am enough! I'm made for a purpose, and I'll be 100 percent me until He takes me home. Until then I will run the race before me, pace myself, and not give up. Rejected Jesus is the cornerstone of my faith. I can do anything through Him who gives me strength."

Week 6
Walk Redeemed

DIRECT MY FOOTSTEPS ACCORDING TO
YOUR WORD; LET NO SIN RULE OVER ME.
REDEEM ME FROM HUMAN
OPPRESSION, THAT I MAY OBEY YOUR
PRECEPTS. MAKE YOUR FACE SHINE ON
YOUR SERVANT AND TEACH ME YOUR
DECREES.
—PSALM 119:133–135

The Steps of the Wise

This is my third try at writing this chapter. Why? Because I struggle with walking redeemed, with what that looks like, and with how I should make wise choices to get to that place. I've not perfected my walk of faith. I don't know what the rest of the path looks like or, beyond finishing this book, what I should do to get there.

It's late 2020. Everyone is struggling financially. Yesterday I applied for a job at my favorite clothing boutique. I've applied for several jobs while writing this book and since my divorce. Although I have everything I need to survive the next couple of months, I still struggle with trusting without doing more. What if I'm being too lazy and should be doing more besides writing? I know God wants me to finish this book, but what if that is not enough? I try to make wise decisions, like what I'll do to pay the monthly bills on my unstable income. Then I wonder if I'm getting off the path God has set before me. I know I'm not trusting He will provide.

How do I talk about walking redeemed when I don't even know if I'm doing it yet? How can I have a strong faith like Ruth, who kept walking with her poor mother-in-law without hesitation? I've surely hesitated many times, thinking, *Which path has the most prosperous outcome?* My discernment involves looking for the easiest and most successful route. I don't want to struggle financially, but I also don't want to go outside of

God's purpose for my life. When there is a fork in the road, I have a hard time deciding which way to go.

Over this entire year, throughout the pandemic of COVID-19, I kept hearing God tell me to get this book revised and completed, but I hesitated. I took on a few extra freelance writing contracts for the income. I took a course to help me grow other areas of my business. Each time I finished something, I'd get the nudge to get back to this book after months of not even opening the document. I found ways to get distracted with a good excuse: I had to make sure I could keep paying the bills. I am weak. I complain when I have to struggle. I want God to provide a perfect path, without curves or roadblocks, to the thriving life He promises. But things don't happen the way I think they should or how I envision them going. I make wrong turns. I make decisions based on what looks like the easiest or best path to follow. I take the fork in the road that loops around right back to where I started. I don't do the things God is clearly asking me to do because I get distracted by earthly things, or I just don't want to, much like Jonah.

But there has never, not ever, been a time when God didn't allow me back on the path He prepared for me. If there is a visual of what this looks like, it's Jesus sitting, patiently waiting at the place where I stopped focusing on this book. He wasn't angry or upset at me. He walked this earth, so He knows the struggle of needing to survive. I may have left the path for a short time to focus on the things of this world, but He never left. He was always there, waiting with expectation of my return, while also loving and guiding me as I moved back toward where I'd left off.

I wisely discerned that I needed to be conscious of the fact that I wasn't promised years to complete this project. I wasn't using my time but wasting it by being focused on the wrong things. Each morning I needed to ask for God's help to renew my commitment to His will for my life and to create time to work on this book, without distractions. And I needed to actively live in the promise and power of God without worry of an uncertain future. Only God knows my last day. Until my final breath, I need to align myself with His wishes and redeem or wisely use the time.

Walking redeemed doesn't have to include earthly riches because my rewards are eternal. It is through God's grace that when I get off the path,

He still is there for me. My faith to walk obediently with Him equals redemption. I may fall short again in the future, but if I keep discerning the Holy Spirit's nudging to continue where I left off, I'm better able to dismiss the deception of the devil, who says, *Are you sure God will really provide for you? Did God really say this is His purpose for your life? What if you're missing out on something better?*

This is true no matter what we are going through or facing. Each of our paths may look different, and we may get off our path many different ways, but God is still sitting here waiting, loving, and guiding us back toward His purpose. He'll keep nudging. He's still here, waiting to continue and restore our daily dependence on Him. We can walk toward that redeemed life He has in store, trusting Him in this.

Going Deeper

READ PSALM 78:11–43 AND PROVERBS 16. DOES ANYTHING STAND OUT?

WRITE OUT PROVERBS 16:21.

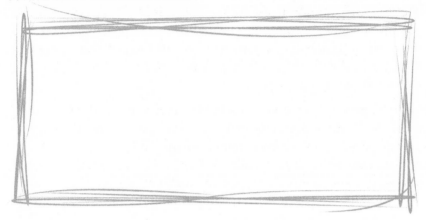

DISCERNING: "Showing insight and understanding."[34]

SYNONYMS

Clear-sighted, insight, intuition, perceptive, vision, wise

AM I USING DISCERNMENT AND SEEKING GOD'S WISDOM FOR HOW HE WOULD HAVE ME PROCEED TOWARD THE REDEEMED LIFE HE PROMISED ME?

AM I TRUSTING HIS LOVE AND GUIDANCE, EVEN IF I MAKE WRONG TURNS OR GO OFF THE MAIN PATH FOR A SHORT TIME?

Biblically Speaking

The Israelites spent a lifetime traveling in the desert toward their promised restoration, as you read in Psalm 78. They forgot what God had done for them and how He had provided; they abandoned their faith for self-preservation and worshipped idols. They were given freedom from their oppression, yet they groaned to go back to Egypt because they didn't know how to step forward joyfully as redeemed people. They thought being abundantly provided for by an abusive pharaoh was better than waiting on God to provide. In their blindness to God's truth, they had trouble discerning right from wrong and fell short of God's Law.

Psalm 78 is the retelling of the Israelites' journey of hardship after God had redeemed them. God provided for them and took care of them, yet they grumbled and turned back to their old habits. In contrast, the Bible shares the joy of walking redeemed. Sorrow and sighing quickly depart from you as you embrace the highway of holiness. The Israelites show you that you are not alone in this human struggle of actively living on the promises and power of God. He still had compassion and mercy for His children when they fell short.

Redemption is the process of redeeming. It is through God's grace and your faith that you are redeemed. The act has already been done to redeem you; it happened on the cross. You've been delivered of your sins, and even of your missteps after. Even with complete redemption, this doesn't free God's people from the devil's schemes to distract, confuse, and misinform. The enemy tries day after day to make you believe God is the deceptive one.

DISCERNING THE TIME

The word "discerning" comes from the Old English word "discerner," meaning "to distinguish between or separate." The act of prayerfully considering the options and what is the best next step is discernment. A discerner deciphers the truth by observing and judging, separating the good from the bad, and trying to choose the right path or the best next step. The Christian life is one of continual forward motion, walking well on good days and not so well on others. That's why the Christian life is a journey to our final destination. All are merely sojourners, traveling until the day we're taken home to be with our Creator.

"Let the one who is wise heed these things and ponder the loving deeds of the Lord" (Psalm 107:43). At different points on this journey you will either walk, run, stumble, crawl, turn away, or refuse to proceed. Pause to discern if you're still on the best path and what will be the next step regularly. Those who are struggling may take two steps forward and one step back, but this is still a forward moving direction. Staying the course means trusting the director of your paths, the Redeemer and restorer of your life.

The journey can become the best part, living in expectation for the good that is to come, even if it's way down the road. Trust that God is not only walking with you but also going before you. Each day is a day to walk redeemed and to redeem the time, seeking His wisdom and direction, thinking through plans, and making sure your choices align with His will. "Look therefore carefully how ye walk, not as unwise, but as wise; redeeming the time, because the days are evil" (Ephesians 5:15–16 ASV).

REDEEMING THE TIME

You have a choice on how to spend the time you have left here on earth. Redeeming the time means being conscious of the fact you may not have another day, so worrying about what you'll need or do weeks, months, and years from now is a useless waste of time. Many people focus on frivolous, earthly pursuits but people of faith focus on their eternal rewards. Having faith in redemption means you know it will happen, but even though you don't know when or how, you stay focused on what's important, using discernment with each step while waiting in expectation.

The steps of the wise discern opportunities. They put away expectations about their current condition and allow God to buy back (redeem) the lost time and opportunities. Your Christian walk is being strengthened and matured as you work through each experience and grow in endurance, even when you take missteps. God wants you to walk with Him in wisdom, growth, and worthiness for your purpose, with all the tools needed for the journey. But even when you go astray, He is merciful to accept you back, still redeeming the time. Each day is another day to renew that commitment to focus on His will.

> Sometimes what we see as wasted time is actually the training ground for what God has in store for us. The lessons we learn and the obstacles we overcome are preparation. Even the rocks you're struggling to climb over today may be the stepping-stones of tomorrow. God never wastes anything. There is great value in where he has led you. And even if you have strayed from his path at times, he's a redeemer who can transform those mistakes into future benefits to you as well. (Holley Gerth, *You're Going to Be Okay: Encouraging Truth Your Heart Needs to Hear, Especially on the Hard Days*)

Don't bide your time here on earth waiting for life to end. Be aware of the ticking clock while making the most of the time. Singleness after divorce is not a jail sentence you count down until you meet someone new or remarry. Time is well spent gaining godly wisdom, seeking His purpose and His will, being in prayer, and examining how you can do the kingdom work God has for you.

Forgiveness Crossing

When I first realized what the Lord had done for me on the cross, I was in my early twenties, with two toddlers. I was invited to attend what I thought was a *group* for single moms, which included dinner and daycare services—who would pass that up? It turned out to be a Bible study. On the first night, being the only one to attend, the group's leader postponed the first lesson to talk with me one-on-one about life as a single mom. She started with sharing her story, which was very similar to mine, making me feel connected and supported immediately. God had redeemed her story and now she was leading this group for single mothers, no matter the reason why we were each single. I didn't see it then, but this was God reconnecting me with His people to learn more about Him. Not growing up in church, I only recall learning about burning in the lake of fire at vacation Bible school at about nine years old. I couldn't comprehend what any of that meant, but I do remember asking God to forgive me and save me from this scary punishment. This group was different.

After that first week, we started our introductory study. It was very basic, with the instruction being about Jesus and His reason to join us here on earth. I learned the cross is important because sin had caused a great divide between God and humans. When He laid the cross down over the divide, it become a walkway for us to reach God and develop a relationship with Him, being immediately forgiven for our sin.

This Bible study was exactly what I needed, when I needed it. If I hadn't been a single mom, I would not have been invited to attend. The fact that it was a needed break from my young babies was all the invitation I needed. Talking to the leader later, she asserted that she told me it was a weekly Bible study when she invited me, but honestly, that's not how I remember the conversation. For some reason, I was deaf to hear exactly what I would be attending. God knew I probably wouldn't have attended if I had really heard what I was coming to. God had chased after and called His one lost sheep to come to Him—*me*! God got me to the class and the rest is His-story. My journey from that first understanding of what the cross means, to the time I spent at a Christian university studying Bible history and theology, and now writing this Bible study, is all part of His plan. I take no credit for the steps I've taken because He has been my guide. We have been walking side by side, redeeming the time together.

Even with what seemed like a detour of marriage and childrearing, then my divorce afterwards, and even when I get sidetracked on other things, they are all still part of my redemption story. Part of this journey was also making stops along the way to release any baggage of unforgiveness for myself that I carried. I can look back and say I should not have gotten married because I'm not really sure if I sought God's will in that situation. I could do that with all the missteps along the way, but instead, I have to choose to accept God's grace and mercy for it all. I am a sojourner who needed to experience all of this to be who He has meant me to be, to bring me to where I am, and to do what He wants me to do, even if that includes earthly consequences like separation from my children or being judged poorly as a divorced woman. What I believe to be missteps are also a part of His plan and purpose.

When I don't let go of what God has already forgotten, I keep myself from experiencing the fullness of life He has in store for me. When I let Satan convince me I should feel shame for what has been forgiven, I stop to see all that as part of the masterpiece that is my life, and I allow that shame to separate me from my loving Father and heavenly Husband. The great thing about knowing God's love, grace, and mercy, and accepting it is the deep understanding that God sees all my secret shame and He loves me anyway.

> Grace means that all of your mistakes now serve a purpose,
> instead of serving shame. (Mike Rusch)

I don't know about you, but after learning that simple fact about Jesus and His reason for dying on the cross—to give us a walkway to our relationship with our Papa, God—I won't let anything separate me from knowing and accepting His love. He has redeemed me, even when I'm just living my life and don't feel very redeemed. I don't have anything substantial to show for this life other than the love and acceptance of my Father, but honestly, that is enough.

Going Deeper

READ PSALM 51 AND LUKE 7:36–50. DOES ANYTHING STAND OUT?

WRITE OUT EPHESIANS 2:8–9.

GRACE: "The free and unmerited favor of God, as manifested in the salvation of sinners and the bestowal of blessings."[35]

SYNONYMS

Compassion, clemency, discharged, freedom, mercy, vindication

IS THERE ANYTHING I NEED TO SEEK REPENTANCE FOR?

DO I NEED TO FORGIVE MYSELF FOR PAST CHOICES OR MISTAKES AND ALLOW GOD'S CLEMENCY TO COVER THEM?

DO I ALLOW GUILT AND SHAME TO KEEP ME FROM WALKING WITH FORGIVENESS AND PURPOSE?

Biblically Speaking

The psalmist David made many missteps along His path as God's beloved and anointed king. His downfall started with something as minor as being in the wrong place at the wrong time (2 Samuel 11). He was supposed to go to war, but he sent Joab instead of going himself. This gave him time on his hands, time for temptation to distract him from the righteous path before him. This started the ball rolling in the wrong direction for David. It led to adultery, murder, and his family being cursed (2 Samuel 12:10–11). These consequences were the effects of sin. Many may see them as punishment or the lack of God's love, but that's not His purpose for the "sword not departing" from his house. Consequences happen because of God's love, not in spite of it; they are His way of disciplining His children. "My son, do not make light of the Lord's discipline, and do not lose heart when he rebukes you, because the Lord disciplines the one he loves, and he chastens everyone he accepts as his son" (Hebrews 12:5–6).

David cried out to God for grace and mercy after He sinned against God and the people he was supposed to protect. He was wholeheartedly repentant of his sins. Through repentance, every sin is forgiven in Jesus. He covers it all with His blood. Although David was not free from the consequences of his choices, he was cleansed of all unrighteousness and could continue to walk redeemed.

Forgiveness is hard. Forgiving someone who has wronged you may take time, but eventually you find mercy in your heart to forgive and move on, with or without that relationship. You work through the anger and grief until you come to accept what has been done. Forgiving yourself is a whole other beast. It is often hard for you to have compassion for yourself. It's hard to let yourself off the hook because you feel you should have known better. This reluctance to forgive yourself not only puts a partition between you and God, but it also stops your emotional growth. Part of walking redeemed is leaving the baggage of being a wretched sinner at the cross. Accepting His forgiveness also means living as you are forgiven.

> When people say, 'I know God forgives me, but I can't forgive myself,' they mean that they have failed an idol, whose approval is more important than God's. (Timothy Keller, *Counterfeit Gods: The Empty Promises of Money, Sex, and Power, and the Only Hope that Matters*)

THE "SINFUL" WOMAN

In Luke 7, a woman living a sinful life approached Jesus with confidence and poured her tears, and possibly her dowry or inheritance (an alabaster jar of expensive oil), on His feet. Back then, when you washed someone's feet, you were putting yourself in the position of the lowest of servants; there's no one lower than a foot washer. She humbled herself before Jesus, which is also a sign of repentance, and washed away the conditions of the world (dirt on His feet from walking in sandals). She used her hair to clean His feet, which was a sign of love. In return, Jesus accepted her and her gracious gift to Him—the anointing of oil and the washing of His dirty feet. Because her sins were greater, she was given more mercy, grace, and acceptance, which caused her to love Jesus even more for what He had done for her—the taking of her heavy baggage. Her sin brought her to Jesus to seek freedom and repentance. She was given complete forgiveness of all her sins.

> The gospel of justifying faith means that while Christians are, in themselves still sinful and sinning, yet in Christ, in God's sight, they are accepted and righteous. So we can say that we are more wicked than we ever dared believe, but more loved and accepted in Christ than we ever dared hope—at the very same time. This creates a radical new dynamic for personal growth. It means that the more you see your own flaws and sins, the more precious,

> electrifying, and amazing God's grace appears to you. But on the other hand, the more aware you are of God's grace and acceptance in Christ, the more able you are to drop your denials and self-defenses and admit the true dimensions and character of your sin. (Timothy Keller)

For some reason, Luke called her a "woman in that town who lived a sinful life" (Luke 7:37) and the Pharisee called her "a sinner" (v. 39). The point is, she was obviously doing something her neighbors knew about to call her a sinner. Although disputed, it's a high probability that this woman was Mary of Bethany, sister of Martha and Lazarus (mentioned in John 12, Matthew 26, and Mark 14). Women in the Bible are often defined by one picture presented, and Luke presented her as a seductress. Yet Mary of Bethany was not known for being a prostitute, and not all sin is sexual in nature, as some believe Luke's text might suggest. Instead, the other gospel writers presented her as a trusted friend of Jesus. Maybe Luke's story was her repentance story.

Maybe these are two different women because there were a lot of Marys and Simons during that time, but the point is still the same. Just like the bleeding woman (in Mark 5), the sinful woman was told her faith had saved her and she could go live in peace, free from the distress she experienced because of sin (v. 50). Grace released her from shame and any torment she may have been putting herself under. No matter who these women were, their stories speak to all hurting and sinful women—the woman you were before you became a true believer, before you knew Jesus and His heart for you and the meaning of the cross (to create a bridge over the divide).

You know why God's commandments are for your benefit, not your restriction? Your sin, even past sin before you were a Jesus follower, caused disharmony. This causes separation. In order to unpack any shame you might be carrying on this journey, you first must be free from the distress that causes you to live without fully accepting His grace. If you haven't left all your heavy baggage at the cross, now is the time to do so. Grace is available for even the most wretched sinners. The more sin you have, the more you realize you need His grace, just like the sinful woman. That darkest secret no one but you and God know about might be holding you back from your emotional healing, and it needs to be brought out into the light. No one is exempt from this. You are not alone in needing forgiveness and grace.

> If we walk in the light, as he is in the light, we have fellowship with one another, and the blood of Jesus, his Son, purifies us from all sin. If we claim to be without sin, we deceive ourselves and the truth is not in us. If we confess our sins, he is faithful and just and will forgive us our sins and purify us from all unrighteousness. (1 John 1:7–9)

*If you need to have a conversation with God to repent of any current or previous sins, know that you'll be sitting with a gentle Father who has nothing but love and grace for you. Ask for His forgiveness and ask Him to direct your paths on a daily basis. No matter what you have done or continue to do, He is waiting for you to come back to Him. He's not waiting for you to clean yourself up before coming to Him because He's willing to wash it all away for you once you accept His grace and mercy.

Unpack Shame

Before I married, I lived with shame. I didn't know it was shame, I just knew I wasn't living right (having children before marriage), and I wanted to do something to correct it. On the day I got married, I thought that would be the end of how I was feeling. I thought I wouldn't have any reasons to feel shame or feel like I was damaged goods any longer. I was now a married woman, a wife, with a husband who was going to take care of me and love me no matter what I had done or would do in the future. He was my savior. But realization set in soon after we were married. Knowing that having children outside of marriage bothered me, so my husband used it against me every time we'd have an argument or each time I found out about his inappropriate relationships with other women, or when he was caught in his lies. He used my shame to keep me trapped in the marriage, just as much as I stayed because I thought the marriage had redeemed my sin. We were both trapped in shame; he just did a better job projecting his inner turmoil onto me.

I thought God had redeemed me when I married. My new husband had been my boyfriend for more than three years, and he was willing to adopt my daughters—making them his own. We broke up for a short time while dating, and in the time between our breakup and the marriage, I became a Christian. He told me he was also a Christian because his grandparents went to church. I thought he had found the cross too because that's what he told me. (Yes, at age twenty-three I was naïve.) He said we were soul mates and that God had brought us back together to spend our life as a family. What a great story to tell our grandchildren! Redeemed and married for life, we'd say. That was always my future hope. I totally bought into the love bombing and empty promises.

After twelve years of marriage, I found out about yet another inappropriate relationship, and I was done. I couldn't keep repeating the cycle of infidelity and abuse. I knew the pattern; there was someone else. He denied it, of course, but by now I was ashamed of all the years I'd wasted trying to defend his character and lack of integrity. All of my misunderstanding of redemption had caught up to me. My useless house of cards that I'd used to hide my shame had crumbled to the ground.

> Shame is life-dominating and stubborn. Once entrenched in your heart and mind, it is a squatter that refuses to leave. (Edward T. Welch, *Shame Interrupted: How God Lifts the Pain of Worthlessness and Rejection*)

During my divorce and in the years since, I've had to unpack and deal with all this unresolved shame. Only a couple of my close friends knew the shame I still carried from before my marriage and how it was used to make me feel worse about myself. Through these healing years, I shared my shame story privately with coaching clients and in private workshops— when they wanted to know how to their release their own shame. Hearing my shame story helped them to realize that what they were feeling was normal, and that speaking about it would help to take away its power over their lives.

Each time I share my story, I gain freedom from my shame. It's part of who I am, but it no longer defines me. I'm not proud of my choices as a young adult, but I am happy all three of my children were given to me to raise, and happy about my two grandchildren (born outside of marriage and created by God). What someone says about me, about the things I've done, no longer hurts me. Their words about me may be true, but I can no longer access any hidden shame because I've left it at the cross.

As a child of God, I'm not shameful to God. I've put my faith in Jesus and what He did for me on the cross. God sees me through my real Savior. That walkway is still there; I can have a loving relationship with Him. Anything I've done and sought repentance for has already been wiped clean. As David put it, "I will not be ashamed when I compare my life with your commands" (Psalm 119:6).

Now I know why God commands that we flee from all sexual sin and refrain from sex outside of marriage—because He only wants what's best for us. He knows the shame we will carry, and how much it hurts our soul to share heart intimacy with someone we're not married to. After totally surrendering my life to God's ways, I find it much easier to live out His commands and live a shame-free life. For this reason, I won't be repeating what led me to carry all my shame in the first place—just like the Samaritan woman. I yearn to be more like Christ and live a sinless life. I will remain virtuous until the day I marry again, if that is God's will for my life.

Going Deeper

READ JOHN 4:1–42. DOES ANYTHING STAND OUT?

WRITE ISAIAH 54:4.

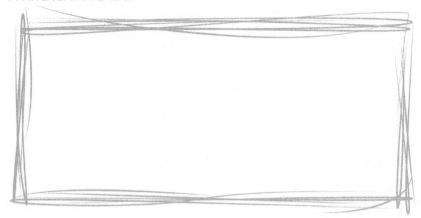

REPROACH: "To criticize someone, especially for not being successful or not doing what is expected."[36]

SYNONYMS

Blemish, disapproval, disgrace, rebuke, shame, stigma

IS THERE ANYTHING HIDDEN THAT MIGHT BE CAUSING ME SHAME?

DOES MY HIDDEN SHAME MAKE ME FEEL BLEMISHED, DAMAGED, OR DISGRACEFUL IN ANYWAY?

DO I FEEL AS THOUGH I WEAR A SCARLET D FOR DIVORCED OR DO I CRITICIZE MYSELF FOR NOT BEING SUCCESSFUL IN MARRIAGE?

HAS SOMEONE ELSE'S REBUKE DEEPLY HURT ME—MAYBE IT CAUSED SHAME?

HOW DOES MY SHAME INHIBIT ME FROM WALKING REDEEMED?

Biblically Speaking

When Adam and Eve felt shame for the first time, they hid and felt fear. Shame causes you to apologize for who you are, your authentic self. It tells you to worry about what other people will think or what they might be saying about you. It makes you feel unworthy and not good enough, so you wear a mask or hide your true self. Shame causes you to put up a wall to keep judgmental people out, but you end up keeping everyone out. You may feel judgment from others who have what you want, even if they're not judging you at all.

> In a futile attempt to erase our past, we deprive the community of our healing gift. If we conceal our wounds out of fear and shame, our inner darkness can neither be illuminated nor become a light for others. (Brennan Manning, *Abba's Child: The Cry of the Heart for Intimate Belonging*)

Jane R. Pennington, MA, wrote a book called *SHAME: Should Have Already Mastered Everything.* The great thing about understanding it this way is reminding yourself that no one has mastered everything. Nobody but Jesus has walked this earth free from mistakes, missteps, or sin. No one. Not one! He was the only One able to master everything, so He's the only human who lived without shame.

When you believe the lie that others have way more figured out than you do, you might think, *Look at all she's accomplished! I have a lot of catching up to do!* You set yourself up for thinking you should have everything they have, that your life is not good enough just as it is or that you should be some place God doesn't currently have you at.

> Shame is the deep sense that you are unacceptable because of something you did, something done to you, or something associated with you. You feel exposed and humiliated. Or, to strengthen the language, you are disgraced because you acted less than human, you were treated as if you were less than human, or you were associated with something less than human, and there are witnesses. (Edward T. Welch, *Shame Interrupted*)

Divorce attacks the sense of identity you got from your core roles, which causes most women to feel shame. Most women grow up believing they'll be a wife and a mother someday, staying married for life, but when an unexpected divorce happens, a woman loses her identify as a wife. And if she doesn't have children, the dream of having them fades away. Those who have children and have to share custody, or if there is a loss of custody completely, strips away the role of being a mother as well. It's understandably hard to share the parenting of your children with another mother, even if you are happy your children have more people who love them. In addition, we believed we would grow old and be accepted forever, no matter how we aged. Now rejected and older, we believe *No one will want me looking like this!*

THE SAMARITAN WOMAN

The Samaritan woman at the well had a pattern of broken relationships in her five failed marriages. She had no husband or headship covering, much like Ruth, and the guy she was with wasn't her husband. Many think she avoided the judgment of other women by getting her water when they didn't—under the noonday sun or at the hottest part of the day (seems reasonable). And at the well she encountered Jesus and His lovingkindness. Jesus revealed and spoke aloud the things she had done and how she was living her life. He brought all the darkness of her past out into the light of the day, where it could be embraced and healed, without criticizing her. The Samaritan woman won the war against her shame when it lost its power over her. It wasn't judgment or reproach that turned her life around; it was grace. There is no condemnation for those who are in Christ (Romans 8:1). God's grace covers what Jesus exposes so you can accept forgiveness.

> This is the last word. Jesus always has the last word, and it is always a good last word. It is always about him and it always takes you by surprise with his love and acceptance. What is your response? John's message is clear: worship him. What does worship him mean? It means everything. It means you turn away from the stagnant pools where you once drank. For the Samaritan woman, it meant she would align her lifestyle with His kingdom. In technical terms, she would repent. She would turn away from acts of death to receive living water, and she would love it. (Edward T. Welch, *Shame Interrupted*)

After her encounter, the Samaritan woman didn't carry the burden anymore. She didn't condemn herself, and she didn't protect those who were also part of her story. Instead, she started the process of breaking free from her shame, and her life was redeemed through bringing others to Christ. Telling your story is how you authenticate who you really are, every piece that makes you *you*. When you deny the truth about yourself, you keep the secrets locked deep inside and they cause disharmony and division. That's a heavy weight to carry around. It weighs you down with shame. That's why you need to unpack it and release it at the cross.

> If we can share our story with someone who responds with empathy and understanding, shame can't survive. (Brené Brown, *Daring Greatly*)

Share your story because all need to be accepted, just like the Samaritan woman. Self-compassion is most important. You're more likely to reach out to someone else who's hurting, to connect and share your experience, if you no longer carry the shame you once did. You gain connection through shared experiences and shared trauma. Someone could benefit from hearing what you've been through, the choices you've made, and how you now walk redeemed.

Don't allow the fear of being unworthy to stop you from real connection with other Christians—a real human need. Being vulnerable is at the heart of the feedback process. It goes both ways, countering with acceptance. Accept all imperfections from imperfect people on earth, especially if they, too, have repented. Another person's judgment is not God's judgment, and your story has value in the kingdom of God.

In order to walk redeemed, you must unpack your shame (even if it's a long slow process). Seek forgiveness and leave all unnecessary baggage at the cross. Jesus is willing to take the load for you; are you willing to give it to Him?

Proceed with Integrity

I didn't grow up knowing about integrity. I'm not sure I even heard that word until I was well into my twenties, maybe even my thirties, and homeschooling my children. I once heard a pastor describe integrity as being more worried about being good than just looking good. Oh yes, I wanted to be good, even if that made other people think badly of me.

It wasn't until the end of my marriage that I realized I was living with someone who lacked integrity. I wondered how I ended up in that position without even realizing who I was marrying. I started to feel less alone after I shared my story on my homeschool blog in late 2014, a year after my divorce was final. It seems many other women, even homeschool moms, realized they were married to someone without integrity as well. They also realized they were stuck in abusive marriages where their husbands had the final say, and their only job was to be "meek," meaning keeping their mouth shut, never complaining, and always putting up with whatever way their husbands treated them or how their men wanted to live their lives.

When deciding if I should proceed with divorce or fight for my marriage, this thought kept coming to my mind: *If I had the chance to do it all over, or if I was going to date a man, would I date and marry my current husband? Would I want to be with a man without integrity?* My answer was no, so I stopped fighting for my marriage and welcomed the divorce so I could live with integrity instead of the facade I was used to.

As I worked through my emotional healing and understood the relationships that had shaped me, I started to take a look at my own character. I learned I had allowed myself to be easily swayed by those in my immediate environment. I allowed my husband to control the dynamic of our home. It wasn't peaceful or even a safe place to be human. I may not have created our family environment, but I certainly didn't do anything to stop it either. In fact, it became very easy for me to go along with the program, to be just as toxic as the person I was married to. Living with people who lacked integrity, having them among friends and family, it became easy for me to have two separate lives. I wanted to walk with God on a daily basis and do His will, and for the most part I did so, but when around friends and family, I was still the person I was before I accepted Christ. I think that even throughout my marriage, I was able to keep these two parts of me separate. My friends and family knew I was a Christian, but they also saw how I still struggled to live a life of integrity. This lack of full surrender caused me to lack peace.

My divorce made it possible for this to change, and I wanted that change very badly. After talking to my therapist at the time, he suggested I start with reading the *Boundaries* books by Dr. John Townsend and Dr. Henry Cloud. I wasn't being my best self because I was allowing boundary pushers to control my life. I was easily swayed, like a tiny bud in the middle of the valley because I didn't have a strong moral foundation in Christ. I wasn't strong in my faith or in my emotional life. I was weak to influence, and that needed to end.

Like I've said, I had been a believer, churchgoer, and a good deeds doer for more than twenty years, but I was not living a life of daily surrender to Christ. I had to give up my peacekeeping (or people pleasing) to be a peacemaker. I had to learn to walk in the power given to me by God. I could open my mouth and speak up when something wasn't right or when I felt someone pushing me to do something I didn't want to do or be a certain way. This has translated to me speaking up more and being my true authentic self. And women actually want to hear what I have to say. I find it amusing that while growing up and all throughout my marriage, I was silenced and told to keep my mouth shut (as I shared in week 3). But now I get paid to empower other women to speak up, share their story, and not put up with abusive men in their lives any longer. I feel that is God's way of redeeming that part of the first forty years of my life. People tried to shut me up, but God said, "No let her speak; she has something important to say." That's redemption!

Going Deeper

READ EPHESIANS 5:1–20 AND JAMES 1. DOES ANYTHING STAND OUT?

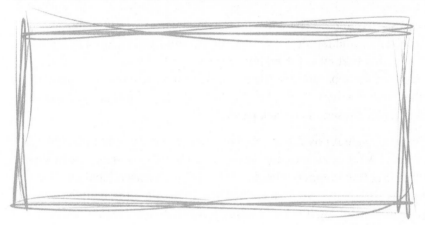

WRITE PROVERBS 10:9.

INTEGRITY: "The quality of being honest and having strong moral principles; the state of being whole and undivided."[37]

SYNONYMS

Forthrightness, being honorable, principle, purity, sincerity, virtue

IN WHAT WAYS DO I STRUGGLE WITH INTEGRITY?

AM I THE SAME PERSON NO MATTER WHO I AM WITH, AND WHEN I AM ALONE?

AM I LIVING AS THOUGH GOD IS IN THE ROOM AT ALL TIMES?

AM I PLEASING TO HIM?

Biblically Speaking

God is omnipresent, meaning He is everywhere at all times. As Adam and Eve learned in the garden, there is no place we can run to hide from Him. There is nothing humans can cover that He won't undercover because He has already seen it. When you're aware of His presence, your freedom is in knowing you are living your entire life in the presence of God.

The Latin phrase *coram Deo,* pronounced core-um day-oh, points out the character of a faithful Christ follower. To live out *coram Deo* is to live before the face of God in His presence, under His authority, and for His glory. It's living in wholeness and unity with your sovereign God. The opposite is to be divided or live a splintered life marked by chaos, confusion, inconsistency, and disharmony. I know that's not you. When a woman is riding the fence and not fully surrendered to God, she's not living *coram Deo.* When she's trying to make friends and family happy, she's not living *coram Deo.*

Integrity is derived from the word "integer," which means "whole." You feel authentically whole by having a synonymous public and private life rather than living a divided life. People who hide certain aspects of their lives often find that God exposes everything in ways they don't want Him to. But when they reveal the truth themselves, God helps them to heal and move forward into righteous living. "Whoever lives by the truth comes into the light, so that it may be seen plainly that what they have done has been done in the sight of God" (John 3:21).

In order to be harmonious within yourself, you must start to put aside all old habits and seek God's direction for your life. God is a God of lovingkindness, watching over you and patiently waiting for you to seek His face. He wants you to live victoriously, but in order to do that, you have to give up what you've always known and be an imitator of God.

"Follow God's example, therefore, as dearly loved children and walk in the way of love, just as Christ loved us and gave himself up for us as a fragrant offering and sacrifice to God" (Ephesians 5:1–2). Other Bible verses say be an imitator of God in all that you do and to be filled with love. That's the key to living a life of integrity while walking redeemed. Be servant-hearted because you know love and are filled with love. You live continually in His presence. As you grow and learn, you don't need to be shackled to anyone or anything earthly because you know you live in the presence of God. You're connected to Him, awaiting your future in His kingdom. Living under divine sovereignty also involves acknowledging the request to give God the glory. Jesus is above all. Everything comes from Him.

In the Presence of God

Not only are you under God's protection and providence, He has also given you a new life to live. In this new life, you have to put to death all the sinful earthly things you used to be in bondage to. Jesus broke those chains for you so you can live free before the face of God—free from your sin and shame. As Jesus put it, "Very truly I tell you, everyone who sins is a slave to sin. Now a slave has no permanent place in the family, but a son belongs to it forever. So if the Son sets you free, you will be free indeed" (John 8:34–36).

If you are free from this enslavement, then why don't you walk free? Why are so many Christians still struggling with sin patterns that include a shoulder load of guilt? For those who aren't stuck in besetting sins, why do they still feel they, too, have fallen short? Because that's how humans feel. Sin was brought in the world. It was in a human's nature and condition, but through Jesus, God's children were put in a position above their sin, above the world, and above the law.

> Tragically, most people spend all of their time (or most of it) focused on their condition rather than their position. (Noel Jesse Heikkinen, *Unchained: If Jesus Has Set Us Free, Why Don't We Feel Free?*)

The enemy wants you to believe your condition is going to be longer than your position. That's a lie! Your permanent position has already been decided at the cross. Once you accept it, you can walk free, knowing it can't be taken away. You are forever in God's favor and your sins have been pardoned.

> Jesus was free because He believed truth in every area of His life (provision, identity, health, power, personal habits, relationships, etc.) We too are to renew our minds to believe truth in each aspect of our lives. As we do, we will take our freedom beyond a meeting and live it out consistently in our lives. Truly, victorious mindsets will make us free. (Steve Backlund, *Victorious Mindsets*)

Don't grow weary of walking in integrity, even while others are getting away with doing wrong. They, too, have the same ever-present God persuading them to turn from their path of destruction to a life of walking with Him. Each human has his or her own path, even those who live divided lives. Your focus should remain on Jesus and the path God has you on, being guided with wisdom from the Holy Spirit.

Until you are stronger in your faith and integrity, you may have to love people from a distance. Work on being so deeply rooted that those who still live a divided life do not sway you. This is your new life after divorce, and you don't want anyone to detour you from your walk with your true Savior. You have renewed your mind to what is truth so you can live a whole, healthy life *walking redeemed.*

Running the Race to Finish

Everything I've done, experienced, and been through could be regarded as a heavyweight suitcase to carry around, or as lessons I've needed to make me who I am today. I choose to believe the latter. I've decided to grow and learn from my experiences, losses, and even the abuse I've experienced. Plus, I don't have enough energy to keep carrying that baggage around with me; it's much too heavy for this woman.

In the past, toxic people just used all that baggage to make me feel even more worthless. They told me I should be ashamed of what I had done, especially before God. Whether it was the enemy using them as a vessel to get to me or their own meanspiritedness, I believed them. My baggage and shame became the enemy's tool to stop me from moving forward, from being emotionally healthy, and from getting to where God wanted me to be. I believed I wasn't worthy of God's anointing or purpose because of all the baggage I carried!

Many times during and after my divorce, I wanted to give up. I wanted to throw in the towel, send my youngest child to live with his dad, and run away to try to escape everyone. I was so tired of carrying the heavy load. I had a hard time watching my ex-husband get away with everything he was doing in broad daylight while I always tried to do the right thing. It seemed so very unfair, and I didn't want to watch. It seemed like he had a great life after divorce while I struggled. Each and every time he did something unfair, my small support group would have to remind me to keep going and keep fighting to regain some of myself and everything that was lost.

Each day is just another day to keep running that race, to keep moving forward. Watching what my ex-husband is doing or not doing is just a distraction from me living my best life. I can't watch the road in front of me while driving if I'm looking out my back window. That should not even be in my view. His choices are no longer connected to me; that's why he's now called an "ex." He has exited my life, and now I'm free to keep looking forward to my redeemed life.

I believe God is within me, guiding my every step through every struggle. He is holding me up when I feel I can't take another day. He won't let me fall, and any missteps on my part will still be part of the bigger picture— His plan. I probably could've had this book finished a year ago, but I stopped for a rest break on this marathon I named "my anointed purpose." God called me to do this work of encouraging and guiding women during and after their divorce, but I stopped and lay down by the side of the road for a while, telling God I couldn't keep going, that I didn't feel prepared for this calling. I told Him it was too hard. I wanted the easiest and most prosperous route, not the route with hard work and the dedication to continue until completion. But doesn't everything good take hard work? In rebuilding and regaining my faith, I've learned that this is running the race set out before me. Even when I feel too weak to move forward toward the goal and want to give up, I have to keep putting one foot in front of the other and depend on God for my strength to keep going. I have renewed my commitment and dedication to do exactly what God has asked me to do. This is His purpose for my life; this is me doing kingdom work that translates into heavenly rewards, even if I don't see them here on earth.

Writing this book is not the end of my purpose. There will be something else God asks me to do (another book, another group coaching course, or something else). Maybe it will be even harder than researching and writing this book has been, but I will still continue to walk in God's will for me and watch Him rework the pain of my divorce into something good. I will continue to keep pressing on until it's my time to go to my heavenly home. I will keep running the race, often pacing myself, to keep myself going for the long haul. It may seem like a lifetime to get to the finish line because it is. It's a lifetime journey, but we're walking with our biggest fan, our biggest supporter—our Savior, Jesus Christ.

Going Deeper

READ 1 CORINTHIANS 9:24–27 AND 2 TIMOTHY 4:1–8. DOES ANYTHING STAND OUT?

WRITE OUT PHILIPPIANS 3:14.

HEAVENWARD: "Directed or moving toward heaven or the sky; upward."[38]

SYNONYMS

Ascend, elevate, escalate, rise, skyward, surmount

WHAT DIRECTION AM I HEADED IN?

WHAT GOAL WILL BE ACHIEVED AT THE END?

WHAT CAUSES ME TO STUMBLE AND WANT TO GIVE UP?

WHO IS WALKING WITH ME?

DO I RELY ON HIM EACH AND EVERY DAY?

Biblically Speaking

You wake up to the sun shining, the birds are singing a beautiful song, and you think to yourself, *Today is going to be a great day!* You have great things planned and you love your new life free from drama, chaos, and oppression. Then one thing happens, and another. You have a grouchy kid who doesn't like the sandwich you packed in the lunchbox. You just realized you forgot to pay a bill and now you'll have to pay the late fee on top of that. You're running late to an appointment. Money is tight. You are really feeling overwhelmed by life. You see things going downhill very quickly and wonder how to get it back under control. *No, no, no, this was going to be a great day—it started so well!* You're so tired of these types of days, and there are a lot of them.

Do you throw your hands up, give up, and quit life? Do you get angry and start throwing things? No, you keep running the race and keep the hope that better days are coming. They are promised! You hold on to the good parts of each day and choose to be thankful, knowing that every day has some good and some bad. Honestly, life is hard. There really is no easy path, although it may look like some people found it when you couldn't.

Paul said, "Let us not become weary in doing good, for at the proper time we will reap a harvest if we do not give up" (Galatians 6:9) and "I press on toward the goal to win the prize for which God has called me heavenward in Christ Jesus" (Philippians 3:14). He wanted to keep the spiritual goal of being in heaven with Christ as the finish line of this race called life. Paul's focus was on forward momentum rather than mistakes of the past. You can't move forward if you're still heavily focused on the past—what was, what happened, or what could have been. There is a time for mourning all of that; then there is a time to leave it all behind to press forward for the days ahead and the future afterlife.

Pressing forward and walking with God doesn't free you from human peril. The Christian life is often rife with danger and uncertainty, even when you mind your own business and just try to survive. Too many things slow you down or distract you. But do not lose heart; Jesus has overcome the world, and one day you will reap the rewards for all you have done. God is not looking for a winner. There is no competition between you and other people. God is just asking you to persevere and have strong faith through the rough times so you can cross that finish line at the end, where everyone gets a crown of glory (1 Corinthians 9:25).

JOY AT THE END

Toward the end of His life, Jesus asked His disciples for help, even though He knew humans disappoint sometimes. Jesus wanted to pray at the foot of the Mount of Olives. He and His disciples had just finished their meal and proceeded to their usual prayer spot. Jesus asked the men to pray and keep watch over Him because He was crushed with grief and needed their support. While they settled in after their big meal, Jesus cried out. "Father, if you are willing, please take this cup of suffering away from me. Yet I want your will to be done, not mine" (Luke 22:42).

The disciples couldn't see what was going to happen to Jesus, what He would have to endure, so in their lack of concern, they repeatedly fell asleep. Jesus knew His time had come; He had run the race with endurance and knew God was taking Him home. The sad news is that Jesus had to die and take the punishment for something He didn't do. The good news is that Jesus died so you (and I) could be forgiven and live in eternity with God. Jesus was walking heavenward. Eternity is the prize at the end of this journey. It is promised to those who believe. Because of the joy that awaited Jesus, He endured the pain, not even worried about the shame. He was being reunited with the Father. Joy can be found in God's presence. Jesus could trust that everything bad from this sinful world would be gone when He arrived at His heavenly home. And the deepest joy comes from knowing all has been conquered, all has been cleaned up and resolved, and none of this pain, fear, or destruction is present in heaven. All of it is wiped away.

To this day you can come to the Lord and find comfort, healing, and faith to endure your own struggles, on the good days and the bad. Heaven will come down to you, through the Holy Spirit, and you will be reminded that you can experience this authentic joy for yourself. "May the God of hope fill you with all joy and peace as you trust in him, so that you may overflow with hope by the power of the Holy Spirit" (Romans 15:13). This is truly something to be thankful for, even during so many struggles (like most of 2020).

> God is within her, she will not fall; God will help her at break of day.
> (Psalm 46:5)

Week 7
How God Has Prepared Me—My Life Has Purpose

THOSE HE PREDESTINED, HE ALSO
CALLED; THOSE HE CALLED, HE ALSO
JUSTIFIED; THOSE HE JUSTIFIED, HE ALSO
GLORIFIED.
—ROMANS 8:30

The Seasons of Preparation

During my divorce, God showed me that everything I had been through would be used for a purpose. He would work it together for good and not the evil it felt like at the time. Romans 8:28 was a verse I saw on repeat all throughout that year my divorce was being finalized. As I analyzed it over and over, I just kept reminding myself *He has a plan, He is my forever Husband, and I'm called according to His purpose.* Nothing was going to separate me from Him again in the way my marriage had.

At the time of my divorce, I was doing some freelance writing as well as writing my own homeschool blog. This was bringing in a small amount of money to help pay a couple of bills. I didn't know how God was going to work out His plan and purpose, but I just kept working on what was in front of me. When someone asked me to work for them, I'd take the job. I spent lots of time in therapy working on my emotional healing. By the end of the first year after my divorce, something felt different. It was as if I'd spent all of 2014 preparing for something, yet I would not say I was actually doing any preparation work beyond the emotional healing. God was working in me; I just didn't know it yet.

It wasn't until late 2014, a full year after my divorce was finalized, that I shared publicly I was now divorced. I felt a nudge that it was time to share this with my readers because it felt like I was living a lie, so, I wrote a blog post on my homeschool blog. I assumed that would be the end of it. Either no one would care or they would all judge me as a sinner for being a divorced woman and stop reading. I was preparing for the latter. I had already felt shunned by the church we had been attending because they were praying for marriage restoration, so I didn't know if I could take any more women telling me I would suffer for the rest of my life because I was now divorced—like somehow I'd gotten myself into this mess so it was my cross to bear.

To my surprise, that one blog post was actually very well received. It was shared many times. I started receiving emails from readers and other bloggers sharing how they, too, had gone through a divorce, either recently or in the past. They shared how divorce, adultery, and abuse in a Christian marriage was not a widely talked about subject. It was so nice that they were willing to bring it all into the light of day, out of the shadows of darkness. I started writing and sharing even more of my experience, which again was well received by mostly everyone. I don't recall hearing much backlash, which was probably good at that time when my fragile self-worth could not have handled anyone telling me to stop writing.

Now, almost seven years later, I'm still talking about these same topics. I receive a ton of resistance and adverse reactions to what I share on the internet. Being rooted in my worth to God (most of the time), rather than having my self-worth dependent on what others think of me, has primed me for being a target of criticism, disapproval, and condemnation. Every few months I get an email from someone who says I'm going to hell for what I do in my ministry. I receive hate mail telling me to repent and stop encouraging woman to divorce. When I talk to other people in ministry, they share that no one is free from this amount or type of rebuke. I'm often tempted to give up when things like this happen because it is hard to take at first, but Jesus went through the very same thing when He walked this earth and ran His race.

To be more equipped to handle my purpose and God's plan, I need to have a Christlike character and the endurance to keep going when things get tough—because they do. Has running my race been easy? No. I've struggled often, especially in the beginning. I struggled when my website went down or I didn't know how a difficulty would be worked out. I wanted to quit so many times, but I had to remind myself that feelings are fleeting, that God had me, and this all had a purpose. I knew that if He wanted me to stop doing this, He would not keep paving the way. Instead, He would've closed the door a long time ago.

Each experience, even the struggles, is another chance for God to prove to my shaky security that He is going to get me through this as well. Each criticism from the outside world is another opportunity to practice trusting Him. I feel His pruning shears as He cuts out people or experiences that have kept me from moving forward on this journey. Some of my friends and family couldn't walk this path with me because they would have distracted and detoured me from my purpose or made me feel like I shouldn't go any further. I didn't get jobs I applied for because they weren't part of the plan and purpose for my life, even when it felt like a personal rejection at first.

As God raises me into my place of His glory, speaking the message He has put on my heart, I feel the wind's resistance and the atmosphere change. I have more negative feedback and more criticism about the work I do and who I am helping. To some divorce is shameful, sinful, and a taboo subject, but God sees the need and the purpose of this ministry. He has a heart for abused and disparaged women. His character and heart have softened my heart for them as well. This helps me to keep going. That's exactly how He wants me to see, and continue to see, the need. Now, any resistance I might receive from the outside world is just a reminder that I'm doing something right because it bothers people today who still think like Pharisees. Little by little I'm being sanctified as I walk out my purpose. A stable character is needed to ride out the intense storms during the seasons of preparation, growth, and purpose. Without my faith foundation and the reminder that this is all for the greater good, I would have quit a long time ago.

I surely didn't get to this place—where I can let go of the criticism and work through struggles—overnight. It has been a long, slow process through each difficulty and triumph. I've had to see how God is using these struggles for my personal and spiritual growth. Looking back at each occurrence, I'm reminded that I've made it this far, and I will make it even further if I don't give up. I'm not a runner, but my life experiences have shown me I can endure this race just as Jesus did. Around the corner will be another example of God coming through, if I just wait patiently for it while walking in my purpose.

> The first step in walking in your God-given purpose is identifying your calling. Your calling is the foundation. It will carry you when times get hard. You will be reminded of it when you want to quit. It may not even make sense at first. But it won't let you go another day without its presence in your heart. (Andrea G Williams, *Ask. Seek. Knock.: 4 Simple Steps to Find Your God-Given Purpose in Life*)

Going Deeper

Read John 17, Ephesians 4:1–16, and John 15:1–17. Does anything stand out?

WRITE 2 THESSALONIANS 2:13.

SANCTIFY/SANCTIFICATION: "To set apart to a sacred purpose or religious use; to make productive of holiness or piety."[39]

"To 'sanctify' something is to set it apart for special use; to sanctify' a person is to make him holy."[40]

SYNONYMS

Appropriate, dedicate, establish, exalt, mature, perfect

CAN I SEE WHERE GOD WILL USE MY LIFE EXPERIENCES, AND EVEN MY TRIALS, TO PREPARE ME FOR MY PURPOSE AND MY FUTURE?

AM I GAINING A STRONGER FAITH AND MATURITY AND BEING
SANCTIFIED AS I PREPARE FOR THE NEXT CHAPTER OF MY LIFE?

Biblically Speaking

The time between the calling of your purpose and seeing God's purpose for
your life is the season of preparation. Even after you are given the call,
there may be a time of enduring to prepare you for the things to come.
Many man or woman of the Bible, including Jesus, had a long period in
their lives when they were maturing and preparing for ministry or their
divine purpose. Jesus was set apart and had to be equipped for the time He
would be tempted by Satan to walk away from God. He was set to endure
the rejection from even those closest to Him who tried to stop Him. He
knew His purpose the entire time, yet He still had to persevere through
those difficult times.

Spiritual growth and maturity take time and effort; this is the sanctification
process. There are no fast tracks or shortcuts through this process of
growing in Christ and in Christlike character. You grow in Him so you can
overcome the world, just as Jesus did. You are chosen as God's beloved
daughter to do His work here on earth. As you read the resource guide (the
Bible) on this journey, you see that to have "the mind of Christ" (1
Corinthians 2:13–16), you must accept His spirit and allow Him to instruct
you. The rest will be deceived and go their own way.

For a few, spiritual growth is a lengthy operation, like farming or
gardening. Any gardener or farmer must prepare the soil before planting
seeds. After this time of preparation, the farmer has to wait for the seeds to
take root and sprout. He (or she) must nurture and protect the earth from
outside troubles, often by putting up boundaries (a fence), or by spraying—

to keep the bugs or animals away. The farmer must stay close to provide the seeds with needed nutrients, sunlight, and water—not too much or too little—for them to grow and mature.

In organic farming, it's important to prune the seedling leaves at the bottom of a new plant once the secondary leaves and flowers bloom. This sends more nourishment to the main plant and allows for focused growth. This is so the tiny sprouted plant is not trying to give energy to the unneeded first leaves. The same is true when a houseplant has a diseased or dead leaf. If you don't prune it from the plant, it will cause the whole plant to die because the plant uses all its energy to save that one dying leaf.

I have a spider plant that has died many times because I didn't prune it enough, and all that was left were the roots. I've also killed a few succulents by overwatering, but I'm learning and growing with each new plant I purchase and try to keep alive.

For the first-time gardener, it will be many years after the first planting season before the gardener sees a typical thriving, yielding crop because with each season of planting, sowing, and reaping, the soil gains more organic nutrients that allow for optimal plant growth. Each year, the gardener will make changes or deal with issues in order to produce more and more fruit and vegetables in the years to come. With each bigger harvest, he must continue to do what he was meant to do, even if a crop fails. He can't give up because a few years are hard. He has to keep plugging away while keeping the faith and work the soil to produce what it was designed to.

The heavenly Father is your gardener. He plans to nurture you so you will grow and mature and become more Christlike, so you will endure, producing more and more fruit each year. Many call this "maturity in Christ," "growing in the Lord," or "experimental sanctification." The first step is to bring you closer to Him—to give you your needed nutrients and to heal your soul. He wants to teach you how to produce the fruits of the Spirit and to know your gifts, and His desire is for you to know how to use those gifts for His purpose. With each new emotional experience, you gain more wisdom to accomplish that purpose.

> May God himself, the God of peace, sanctify you through and
> through. May your whole spirit, soul, and body be kept blameless
> at the coming of our Lord Jesus Christ. The one who calls you is
> faithful, and he will do it.
>
> —1 Thessalonians 5:23–24

BRAIN MATURITY

In biology and psychology, while a child is maturing, the brain prunes the
synapses (little junctions) between nerve cells to allow for better output.
This happens because these junctions are no longer needed for the fully
mature person. Adults need to store more information and make wise,
responsible decisions with the possible consequences in mind. Synaptic
pruning is influenced by environmental factors and is connected to
learning. A mature human can respond to the environment in an
appropriate manner, whereas a child can't make these mature connections.

Mature humans have gained humility, sought wisdom, and learned to
establish their values and standards separate from those of their parents.
They become less of a selfish child and more of a humble individual ready
to serve humanity. In the Bible, maturity is referred to as having a
Christlike character or behavior through a renewed mind and tested faith.[41]
A mature Christian woman is well prepared for her divine destiny. She
stays connected to the source of all nourishment and is continually
renewed by the Spirit.

The Bible gives you many troubleshooting instructions for changing the
inside of the garden as well as its outside environment. Do you need a
fence? Yes, during the early days you might need more time away from
certain people and to be sheltered, so He covers you with His protective
cloud of glory. It may seem dark, but it is to keep you safe and to nurture
you with His healing comfort. After a time of healing, He brings you out
from under His wing and into your restored and redeemed life. While
being sanctified, He wants you to have an open-minded, teachable heart.
He wants to develop the fruit of the Spirit. Faith brings joy. Joy in the Spirit
is encouraging and calls you to a greater life. During this maturation, you
are gaining wisdom, nutrients, and gifts as God demonstrates His
lovingkindness to you and for you, while forming pathways in your mind
that prepare you for the long journey ahead. There will be pruning, testing,

waiting, and restrictions. You are being set apart and established to be productive.

Your influence may be limited while you're being sanctified, but it's only temporary. Down the path are bigger and better things. God has amazing plans and a purpose for you. The Spirit enables you, not a pastor or teacher. The more you allow Him to mold you, your heart, and your mind, and to ordain you for this purpose, the easier it will be for you to walk in your destiny and move past the difficulties that are sure to come with this divine position. All of your experiences and hardships have led you down the path to your purpose, but you will be in unity with the Spirit so nothing or no one can entice you away. Your life no longer belongs to you, only Jesus. You are one of His disciples on the path to do great things for the kingdom of heaven.

Trusting in God's Timing

During my season of preparation, and even now, I had to learn new responses to life's biggest trials—not easy for this highly emotional girl! Before some faith, maturity, and sanctification, I often thought I needed to figure everything out on my own, especially when I didn't see what I thought should be happening come about as quickly as I thought it should. I thought I was supposed to have it all figured out or at least know where I was supposed to be. I'd ask for help or advice from others farther down the path, wanting that to either solve my problem or get me to where I thought I should be. I'd usually take their advice; might as well try—right? I always felt I should be doing something, not waiting on God to do things for me. I had heard the saying that God helps those who help themselves so I always acted on it, even though it's not written anywhere in the Bible. Prayer was my last choice instead of my first. Stressing and toiling to force a resolution, or trying my hardest to make things right, proved to be a disastrous way of trying to accomplish things, as I was often just messing things up. I didn't understand that if I was just patient enough, things would be worked out perfectly, although maybe not necessarily my way.

For example, when I wanted something or thought I really needed it, I would make it happen. When my (now ex-) husband and I planned to buy a new vehicle, I picked out what I wanted and then planned and figured out how I would get it without looking at all the terms of the loan. In our early twenties, we signed the papers to a vehicle trusting we were getting the best deal, only to learn later that we didn't get an expected discount. Now I don't push forward with my way, getting ahead of the process. When buying my current car, I got preapproved online for a vehicle loan first, looked for a vehicle that fit my price range (seriously), and made sure that it was God's will instead of my own.

As hard as it is, I've learned to find peace, even when I'm waiting for an answer or resolution. I've spent a lot of time in this position over the last couple of years. Peace in this process is truly what I want, even if old habits are hard to break because they are familiar. It takes practice to trust God and His timing every single time without interfering. I have to trust that when I hand over a challenge to God to resolve, I should not take it back. I've given it to Him and I need to trust He is working things out, even if I can't see what He is doing or what's up ahead. Otherwise my life was will go back to being full of stress and chaos.

I still often get off the path and have to go back to where I left off and unite with Jesus again, but He stays on my case as closely as a daily fitness trainer. Just this morning he led me to John 11. After reading this story of the delay of Lazarus's resurrection, I knew these were the verses that best represented this principle of waiting on God's timing. I can trust in God's timing because He has lovingly fashioned every minute of my life into His kingdom plan. What I think is me getting distracted is often Him working things out in me. He's always teaching me something new, and I've even shared some of the new things I've learned in this book. God is working this all out in me so I can share it with you in His perfect time.

My earthly eyes only see what I can see, and my brain only reminds me of what I already know up to this point, but I'm always learning. He's working out my purpose, plan, and position in His kingdom. I can grow and mature knowing God will provide all I need when I need it, direct me when I need direction, and tell me which way to go. He'll open doors that need to be opened and close doors that need to be closed. This book has gotten into your hands only by God's divine power to make things happen the way they're supposed to happen and at the exact right moment—for your kingdom purpose. I still have readers contact me four years after my first book was written to say, "I found you and your book at just the right time." That is God's timing—right when it's needed.

I can fill my mind with worry about how or if things will be worked out, but it is only a waste of my time, energy, and peace. And even when bad things happen in the future, I have His assurance that I will not be consumed by any trial either. I will not be ruined by any storm or consumed by any struggle. He always has every situation inside of His control; I just have to trust Him. Waiting is hard, but it is worth it. And if I need to be some place in life, God will get me there in His perfect timing. With Him, I can get through anything life or whatever the enemy tries to throw at me.

When I think back over my entire life, I'm reminded there has never been a time that hasn't worked out. He always took care of things when I allowed Him to direct my paths. Things might not have gone the way I thought they should, but every single troubled time had a resolution. Every single misdirection turned me back in the right direction eventually. Everything that came my way was part of the bigger picture of my purpose and position in this world. I can either do things His way (full of peace) or my way (full of troubles). I might still end at the same destination, but His way is always better and a lot more peaceful of a journey, and I like peace over chaos, for sure.

Going Deeper

READ JOHN 11 AND 2 PETER 3. DOES ANYTHING STAND OUT?

WRITE 2 PETER 3:8.

POSITION: "A particular way in which someone or something is placed or arranged; A situation or set of circumstances, especially one that affects one's power to act; A person's point of view or attitude toward something."[42]

SYNONYMS

Alignment, arrange, consequence, implement, perspective, situation

HAVE I CALLED GOD TO COME AND HELP WITH A DIFFICULT SITUATION, YET I'M STILL WAITING ON HIM TO ARRIVE?

DO I CONTINUE TO PRAY FOR A RESOLUTION, YET NOTHING HAS CHANGED?

HOW CAN I LEARN TO BE MORE PATIENT AND KNOW GOD'S TIMING IS ALWAYS RIGHT ON TIME?

Biblically Speaking

There are only three documented requests for Jesus to save the day, and each time He didn't respond immediately. The first was when Jesus's mother asked Him to change water into wine at Cana. The second was when Jesus's mother and brothers were outside calling for Him to quit preaching and come with them (Mark 3:21,31–35). They wanted to control

Him and what He was doing, but Jesus knew His ministry was His life calling rather than kowtowing to His family. Believers were His spiritual family, not His birth family. Side note: This is a great reminder that even Jesus ignored His doubting family's requests sometimes. The third was when Lazarus was dying.

"Lazarus" or the Greek form, *el-azar*, means "God helps." Jesus loved Lazarus and his sisters, Mary and Martha (John 11:5). Jesus was their help, even if it didn't seem so at times in the Bible: When Lazarus was sick and dying, Jesus didn't leave immediately and run to him; instead, He stayed in Bethany for two more days. Lazarus had been dead and in his tomb for four days before Jesus arrived: one day of travel for the messenger, two days waiting, and another day of travel to Bethany.

Once Jesus arrived in Bethany, we can almost hear the disappointment in Martha and Mary's words exclaiming that if He had gotten there sooner, their brother would not have died. They didn't understand why Jesus had taken so long to show up when they had sent for him in time. They questioned His love because they couldn't see the endgame, the purpose of His delay. Jesus saw the plan and purpose while the sisters saw the circumstances in front of them. With their earthly eyes, Mary and Martha could only see their dead brother, gone for four whole days, and felt no hope anymore—they thought his soul had left his body after three days. Martha trusted Him though. She knew Him as the Son of God, with the power to do what He wanted in this situation—to make the best choice for the best outcome. She acted in a mature and sanctified way, but she was honest too. She showed her authentic self and Jesus still loved her 100 percent because *He understood her grief.* Jesus was deeply moved as well, weeping over His dear friend's death and full of compassion for his family. Jesus felt grief, and He allowed Himself to feel all of it. He didn't shove it down so He could look like He had His act together. He didn't shove it down even though He knew death was about to lose its power. He grieved openly.

Jesus knew "the Lord has established his throne in heaven, and his kingdom rules over all" (Psalm 103:19). Jesus asked the Father to show His divine power and purpose to all who were watching, to hear His prayer to bring this dead man back to life (v. 42), and God did. He resurrected

Lazarus from the grave. This was a huge miracle no one could deny. It proved yet again that Jesus was the Messiah, God in the flesh, just as everyone said He was. It also proved that not all delays are denials; they are often landing pads for His greater purpose to be revealed.

Jesus's delay was part of the kingdom story, the redemption story. The resurrection of Lazarus proved the claims of Jesus and effectively caused His death sentence—the priests and Pharisees collectively decided Jesus must die. Time is irrelevant to God yet often purposeful. The kingdom's purpose was that Jesus had to die to show His love to the entire world, not just Lazarus and his sisters or those watching that day.

Humans see the circumstances before them, but God sees the bigger picture of how circumstances need to be positioned so His will can be done on earth. God views your circumstances from His position in heaven, above all and overseeing all. He doesn't send you into danger or troubled times. He goes with you. Your circumstances are only temporary, even if Jesus delays in coming to the rescue you expect right away. Ask Him what to do next and then give up control, trusting Him to provide understanding when you need it. In the meantime, rest with expectation. Learn, grow emotionally and spiritually, and establish your environment for optimal growth so God can put you into your divine position. Your purpose is established and secure; it won't be gone before you are ready. The world will be ready for you when it's your time, in His time. Those who believe will see the glory of God.

> He has made everything beautiful in its time. He has also set eternity in the human heart; yet no one can fathom what God has done from beginning to end. —Ecclesiastes 3:11

I Am Anointed

Exactly two months before my divorce was final, a friend and fellow divorced woman invited me to a Wednesday night ladies' Bible study at the church I'd been attending since my separation, not feeling comfortable attending the same church as my husband. The study they were doing— *Anointed, Transformed, Redeemed* by Priscilla Shirer, Beth Moore, and Kay Arthur—was a video and workbook series about the life of David. Honestly, I thought all I would learn was a little more about the life of David to share with my ten-year-old, homeschooled son. I found it hard to find time to do my own Bible study, so I was looking forward to it. I now know God was using it to open the door to the next chapter of my life and the next stage of the plan and purpose He had for me.

Reading back through the pages of that workbook, I can see my deep pain and grief over the loss of my marriage and the life I had planned. I didn't trust that God would work things out for good or that He was giving me hope or a future (Jeremiah 29:11). Like many other women, I felt that I was being punished for things I had done before my marriage or during my marriage. It was all my fault. I didn't deserve anything good. My life was being destroyed (very normal feelings during that time), and I was being rejected. The rest of my life was ruined. How could He use me for ministry to others? My divorce didn't feel like part of a plan. And I was sure only bad things would happen once I became a divorced woman.

But right away, the study talked about being chosen by God, discipled by the Holy Spirit, and loved by Jesus. What a huge difference from what I was feeling! This was exactly what I needed to hear, so I started listening. I wanted to know more. Each week, I learned a new thing about being anointed—handpicked, established, beloved, and positioned by God. This was how God felt about David, even after all he had done. He even called him a man after God's own heart. I started to think maybe I was too. I started to hope there would be a future for me beyond troubles, struggles, and more heartache.

Still very early on this journey, my divorce not even being final yet, I felt this was God saying, "I anointed you for a purpose, and your divorce needs to happen so you can take this divine direction." As I've said before, there would be no way I would be doing what I'm doing, sharing all I share online and in my books, if it wasn't for my divorce. Now, seven years later, after seeing how God prepared me to encourage and empower Christian women through their destruction of divorce, I know I was anointed for this exact purpose. I didn't have kingdom sight at the time. I saw things through my earthly eyes, looking at the circumstances in front of me, but that didn't stop God from pulling me forward on my journey. Like Jesus's family, my family thinks my ministry is crazy, and they often want to control me and get me to stop, but my family is not part of this journey. I kept walking with Him and He has brought me to this place. He will bring you out of your hopelessness and into Himself too. You can trust Him. Just keep walking.

I wasn't given the full picture, but during those early days, God gave me a vision of myself standing on a big stage, speaking to a large crowd. Right away I shut that down. *Nope, not something I enjoy doing.* As an introvert, I told God there was no way I would want to do that. I stumble with my words, with lots of *uhs* and *umms*! I can't speak right and stand up in front of two people, let alone a large crowd of people. I listened, but I was honest with Him and told Him I doubted it. Then I let it go to continue on my journey.

In 2016, almost three years after my divorce, God told me to start a YouTube channel to practice speaking in front of other people. I started a channel, but then I did nothing else. It took a full year of God and many others telling me to start creating videos before I published a few horrible (to me) videos on it. It wasn't easy for me at all, but I kept putting out more videos to help women through their divorce and healing. Through that channel and a couple of public speaking opportunities, I've gotten better (not perfect, definitely still a work in progress) at learning this skill. Now, although I still don't love being in front of a camera, I'm much more comfortable doing what I need to do, knowing it helps women feel less alone. And for the most part, my videos are well received.

Even now, I often think someone else has more skills than I do to create videos or to write articles or books. I didn't know how I could write this book of encouragement when I needed these same words myself somedays just to get through. I've mentally disqualified myself from writing so many times—*I can't write; there are way too many grammar and spelling errors; what will I even say?* He's overridden every excuse and even sent me a few great editors who make my writing look very professional. He doesn't seem to want to take "yeah but" for an answer!

I don't feel prepared, but I was called. And God continues to prepare me for the purpose He has anointed me to fulfill. I was anointed to do many things. This is one of them. He didn't ask me for permission to create His purpose for me. He knows what He's working with and He seems to be okay with it. He's doing the work.

> An author can pen a book without the anointing, but only the anointed author can write words that carry the weight of God to accomplish eternal purposes in the lives of readers. (Priscilla Shirer, *Anointed, Transformed, Redeemed*)

Going Deeper

READ EXODUS 3 AND 4:1–17, 2 CORINTHIANS 1:12–24, AND 1 JOHN 2:18–29. DOES ANYTHING STAND OUT?

WRITE OUT 1 JOHN 2:27.

ANOINTING: "Spiritual anointing with the Holy Ghost is conferred also upon Christians by God."[43]

SYNONYMS

Advance, chosen, consecrate, ordain, promote, set apart

WHAT HAS GOD ANOINTED ME TO DO?

HOW DO I FEEL ILL EQUIPPED TO ACCEPT THIS DIVINE PURPOSE FOR MY LIFE?

HOW CAN I TRUST HIM AS HE DIRECTS AND PREPARES ME?

Biblically Speaking

David was anointed king of Israel at the young age of fifteen, but he wasn't crowned king for another twenty-two years, finally fulfilling the purpose he was called to carry out. While he waited, David was on the run from King Saul and fearing for his life. What a horrible yet humbling experience while he waited! God was his portion, and David knew his position in God's plan, even if it wasn't happening as quickly as one would think it should.

After Saul died, David asked the Lord what He should do (2 Samuel 2). Then he waited until he had God's permission and his anointing rather than just going and taking the position as king. He waited and listened for God's direction. It must have been hard to seek God and wait a little more when David could see clearly God's plan coming to fruition. It was so close, but he waited a little bit more. David trusted God for His perfect timing instead of imposing his own.

After spending forty years shepherding in the desert, Moses, at the age of eighty, was given the opportunity to fulfill his purpose and lead God's people out of Egypt. But Moses didn't jump to do this, actually asking God if He could send someone else (Exodus 4:13). Moses felt he wasn't prepared or equipped enough to do what God was asking of him. He told God he couldn't speak well enough to go in front of the pharaoh. He felt he needed more than just God. But the God who designed him said He would empower him to speak. "The Lord said to him, 'Who gave human beings their mouths? Who makes them deaf or mute? Who gives them sight or makes them blind? Is it not I, the Lord? Now go; I will help you speak and will teach you what to say'" (Exodus 4:11).

Many Christian leaders and pastors say they were anointed to preach, heal, or prophesy. When someone does great things via ministry or has a large platform of followers, people think he or she is anointed to fulfill that purpose. That can be true and false at the same time. The truth is we are all anointed to fulfill a purpose as long as we are following Jesus, have accepted the Holy Spirit as our guide, and do this in God's timing.

Seeking, waiting, and listening to God's leading might be difficult for you. You might get ahead of God, or seek human acceptance and your earthly importance rather than God's acceptance and the kingdom's work. Even David struggled with the power that being a king gave him. He took Bathsheba when she was not his to take *just because he could.*

Another struggle those in ministry have is thinking there is not enough anointing to go around. What if God anointed only one person for a purpose and then He couldn't anoint another person for the same purpose? Just because God gives one person a divine destination doesn't mean He won't give another person the same destination. One person's large ministry doesn't stop God's purpose for another person. Some women have ministries that serve thousands or millions; another woman may have a ministry that serves one person at her local church, like the woman who introduced me to Christ and the cross. You, too, have a position to fill. No one is above or below you in anointing; it's not based on your wealth, personality, numbers, or prestige. It's all about God's purpose for your life.

Being anointed is being divinely appointed; it's the act of anointing that sets you apart to complete your call. You are Spirit-filled when you invite and receive the Holy Spirit in faith. You are anointed by the heavenly Father, and His spirit anoints and activates your gifts so you can complete everything God has written in the book of life He has about you. He just asks you to remain in Him and keep doing whatever He asks you to do.

MOSES'S PURPOSE

Moses was called before he was prepared (Exodus 3). What Moses hadn't quite realized is that God doesn't base His choice of who to anoint on their resume of being well prepared with the right words or the right tools. No, God prepares and instructs those He has chosen. God created you and decided your purpose, and then the Holy Spirit sanctified and enabled you to do whatever God has called you to do. He provides the needed gifts and establishes you; you're handpicked and directed into your times of preparation and the fulfillment of your purpose.

Moses was anointed to bring the Israelites out of Egypt, receive the commandments for God's people, and stay with God's people in the desert, yet he was in preparation mode for most of his life before he began his kingdom work.

When you do not see anything happening, it could be because God is doing more in you than through you at the moment. He has to work on you—your heart, your patience, and especially your obedience for His work—before He'll reveal the destination in full detail. He's preparing the details you cannot yet see because you're not there yet. You never have the full picture of what's coming in the future, what will happen, or how things will play out, but you might have a general idea. However, this story isn't only about you—you'll never fulfill your purpose alone. He's preparing other people to walk alongside you, to complete the bigger picture. We all have needs; we all have a purpose. All His children will eventually come together to fulfill many purposes. In every season He is connecting you to the right people, the right lessons, and the right experiences so that you'll be a huge blessing when He needs you to be.

In the in-between, while you're waiting, God is your guide and protector. He has given you a destiny, an inheritance, and a legacy, even if you don't know what it is yet. You didn't take missteps by getting married or divorced; your legacy is not tied to any one person here on earth. Your legacy is tied to the good you will do and the divine plan God has for your life. Just as there is a season for everything, there is a season to wait, to seek His guidance, and to rest in Him.

God knows more about what you need and when you need it than you do. He knows when you will be prepared and when He will need to move you into position. He legitimizes, supports, and sustains His children—those who love Him and are called according to His purpose (Romans 8:28). Even when life seems to be going nowhere and the past looks like a mass of destruction, God is working things out according to His kingdom plan. The waiting period or delay is not a denial of help. He will make the way clear. "What he opens no one can shut, and what he shuts no one can open" (Isaiah 22:22). You are His daughter, with divine empowerment and the ability to do good work as His faithful servant. Nothing or no one can take that away. Be conscious to what He would have you do, where He would have you go, and how you will serve His ministry. That's how you become part of His divine story (His-story).

Jesus touched lives and performed miracles. He knew the connection between the benefits, the requirements, and the responsibility of being God's anointed. You have access to the same power He did and the same responsibility of obedience. Jesus's death tore the veil of separation between you and God. You now have access to Him every minute of every day; there is no need to see a priest or give a sacrificial offering to connect with Him. Keep spending time with Him worshipping, listening, renewing your heart and mind, and putting your faith in action. When you feel doubt, ask God to assist you in your unbelief (Mark 9:24).

> If you look at your circumstances you will put off doing what God is telling you to do. It can seem like the worst time to do whatever God says to do. *But* there is an anointing on 'now' if God has told you to act. (Joyce Meyer, *Beauty for Ashes: Receiving Emotional Healing*)

Using My Gifts

I grew up believing I was an extrovert because I enjoy getting to know people through talking to them at length. I've always had something to say. I'm also often not shy, especially after I get to know someone. But the fact is I'm still introverted. It was after I took the Meyers-Briggs Type Indicator, a personality test, in college that I understood why I enjoy deep conversations with small groups of people and why I needed alone time to recharge after.

Also, at some point early in my marriage, I started to realize I had a spiritual gift of discernment—of people and spirits. When I met people, I often could discern their motives right away. (Yes, too bad I was already married. I would have noticed the red flags.) My former husband hated my intuition and how I could read a person. Each time we'd meet someone new, he'd say I was going to ruin things by listening to that gut feeling (what we called it at the time). He also hated the dreams I had that told me things were happening or about to happen. To protect my relationship and marriage, and to make him happy, I started to ignore the visions and my senses, pretending they didn't exist.

Shortly after my divorce, and after learning I had an anointing from God to use my divorce for good, I knew I needed to know my unique spiritual gifts and how they would be used to help others. The first step was taking a spiritual gifts test, so I asked my pastor for a copy. When I got the results, I was shocked to find that the things I was denying were gifts from the Spirit—teaching, exhortation (encouragement), discernment, and prophecy. During my time of healing, personal preparation, and emotional and spiritual growth, I've been able to develop these gifts again, using them for good. And as much as many people, including my family, don't appreciate my gifts, I know they have a purpose in the kingdom.

Several people have asked me how I know which dreams and visions are real. Most often they're not in line with how I would envision things—they are very different to the way I think, so that's a huge hint as to whether or not one is from God. The dream might show me what will or might happen. During my marriage, I had dreams my husband was having an affair before I knew it was happening. I knew it was a confirmation from God, but I still didn't want to believe it. I didn't want it to be true. And as much as I tried, I couldn't stop the affairs from reoccurring, yet God had the kindness to prepare my heart for the pain. That's why I feel I relate so much to Joseph's story and the gifts God had given Him (in Genesis).

God also designed me with the spiritual gift of teaching. I have the Holy Spirit-led ability to read, properly interpret, and teach the concepts of the Bible. Without this gift, I'm unable to fully accomplish my calling to encourage and empower Christian women through their divorces so they can thrive afterwards. I love when I share the real meaning behind a passage, such as Malachi 2:16, when a woman has only heard opinions of what Malachi meant through a judgmental filter. I share God's heart for His daughters rather than what we often feel is the condemnation of God when someone utters, "God hates divorce! Period!"

Am I perfect at using my gifts? No, but I use and develop my talents each time I write an article or a book that includes my study of the Scriptures, especially when I write about divorce and healing in the aftermath. It's all about growing and learning as I keep preparing for what's next in my life's purpose. I have kingdom work to do. It's work I'm anointed to do, and God is always preparing me for what's next while I continue to follow His direction. My gifts are just the tools I need to accomplish His kingdom work. They also show me I was created uniquely for this purpose and position; it wasn't me taking something that didn't belong to me. It is through my faith and His direction I'm able to keep writing and speaking out, sharing what He has done and continues to do for me.

I continue to hone my spiritual gifts. You can too.

Going Deeper

READ ROMANS 12:1–8 AND 1 CORINTHIANS 12. DOES ANYTHING STAND OUT?

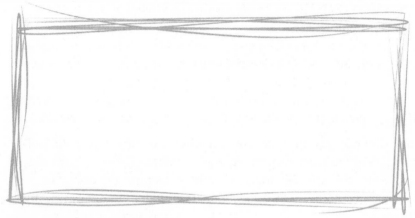

WRITE OUT ROMANS 12:6.

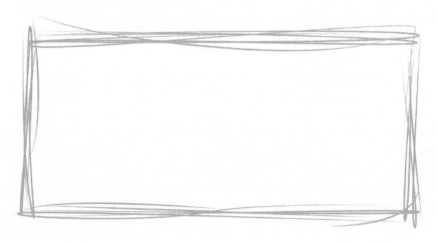

SPIRITUAL GIFTS: "A spiritual gift is a supernatural ability given by God to the believer for the purpose of serving; may be a God-given talent that is directed by the Holy Spirit."[44]

SYNONYMS

Ability, attribute, benefit, conferment, endowment, talent

TAKE YOUR SPIRITUAL GIFTS TEST AT SPIRITUALGIFTSTEST.COM, IF YOU HAVEN'T ALREADY DONE SO. LIST THEM BELOW.

IN WHAT WAYS HAS GOD IDENTIFIED AND DEVELOPED MY DIVINE ABILITIES?

IN WHAT WAYS HAVE I DENIED THESE GIFTS?

HOW CAN I BETTER HONE THESE ABILITIES GOD HAS BLESSED ME WITH AND USE THEM FOR MY DIVINE PURPOSE?

Biblically Speaking

The church is made up of the entire body of believers (those who believe the Lord created the earth, came to earth as a human, died on the cross to pay the debt for sin, and then sent the Holy Spirit to guide them) and not just the people who attend a weekly service in one building, set of buildings, or a denomination. Just as the human body has a purpose for each part, so does the body of Christ. Each individual has a part to play in the life of the church body. Through the Spirit, each believer is given a unique set of gifts to perform their divine tasks. These gifts are for you to fulfill your purpose and to do God's kingdom work. He wants you to use what He has given you.

Paul wrote to the Romans about their salvation through grace and their belief in Jesus Christ as their Savior (Romans 1–11). Then he told them what they could do because of receiving God's mercy (Romans 12). You can offer your body as a living sacrifice. You will never be able to repay God for what He has done, and He doesn't expect it, but you can show your love to Him by being part of His kingdom work here on earth. You can be His hands and feet to continue the work of Jesus through the guidance of the Holy Spirit. Do so with diligence. Walk with Jesus. He will give you the gifts and reveal the purpose you are to use them for.

The reason Paul wrote to the people of Corinth about spiritual gifts was that they were not using them for what they were intended. They were pretending to speak in tongues when they didn't have that gift. And some were asking why some Christians were not given spiritual gifts because some gifts didn't seem as spiritual as others. Paul was putting the people of Corinth to task by reminding them of their purpose and worth in the kingdom of Christ. He was letting them know all gifts are spiritual because every Christian who truthfully and sincerely says "Jesus is Lord" has the Holy Spirit, therefore everything we do has His spirit running through it.

Spiritual gifts come in all varieties, and each believer is given a different set of gifts to serve others. These gifts are from God and should be used for the advancement of Christianity, not for selfish reasons or to gain power. They're not to bring status or respect to an individual but to bring glory to God. Humans were designed to encourage and empower others. Let love be the motivating factor and use your gifts to serve others, just as other Christians use their gifts to serve you. These Spirit-filled gifts are used to serve the church. "Each of you should use whatever gift you have received to serve others, as faithful stewards of God's grace in its various forms" (1 Peter 4:10).

We all need each other, and by serving each other with our unique set of gifts, we'll build a strong local or online family of believers who can glorify God together, all being blessed as a result. Each person's gift(s) fits with others to form the whole, to make the church work the way it was designed to. Each gift holds equal value; a pastoral or teaching gift is no more important than the gift of faith, mercy, or hospitality. Each gift serves a purpose, working with all the gifts for the one common goal of being the body of Jesus on earth. Amputees will verify they don't function the same with a missing body part. We need each other.

Your guide, the Holy Spirit, has given you gifts so you can be an effective participant in the church body. Each part cannot be effective unless all other parts are participating and honored for their role. God may be developing your gifts, especially if they are not yet natural to you. Ask others to pray and support you in your season of preparation, as you accept and develop your unique set of gifts.

> We are fellow workmen (joint promoters, laborers together) with and for God (1 Cor 3:9 AMP). You know you can do nothing apart from Him. You know 'we were all given the one Spirit to drink' (1 Corinthians 12:13 NIV), and when we drink from His Spirit He abides in us and we abide in Him. With that as our foundation, we

can talk about collaborating with God. (Eddie Summers, *50 Shades of Grace (Christian Life): Free at Last)*

Honing your spiritual gifts, natural talents, and, of course, your passions is important to your life and your purpose. First, seek God in how to hone in on your gifts and learn to accept them. Ask Him to show you ways you can develop them without denying them or being tempted to use them to corrupt or manipulate others; no one is immune to this as the devil is always seeking to destroy Christians, their gifts, and those who need them the most.

Search for mentorship from others with the same or similar gifts. Seek to learn all you can about the gifts you know you've been given. Study others and their use of spiritual gifts. Observe how they are unique in their use of their gifts and how they're the same as others. And seek God as to how He would have you grow your gifts so you can use them in your unique way. He designed you in such a way that your gifts could be used for a unique purpose, a purpose only you could pursue and fulfill. In His time, you'll walk forward doing exactly what you were meant to do. Just stay vigilant. The devil will persistently try to entice those doing great things for the kingdom to go against God and seek to fulfill selfish and evil ambitions with their gifts. Stay in prayer to be protected from the Evil One, and pray for others who are using their gifts for the glory of God.

Beginning of Something Amazing

In the many years since my separation and divorce, I often see how God relishes in showing off His all-knowing, all-seeing, and ever-present power with things relating to my purpose. This was very evident when I wrote my first book, *You Can Survive Divorce*. I had no idea how I was going to take those 25,000-plus words from my journal entries and notes and make a book out of all of them. Beyond college writing and blog posts, I had never put words together to form a nonfiction book, and definitely not a book anyone would want to read.

I knew nothing about book publishing beyond that I would need help, especially from a good editor. Just a short time after I started asking around in writing groups, I was in contact with Sally, my editor. She told me to send her a chapter and she'd show me what she did. It was then I knew I needed to hire her. She took my B- or C+ work and made it A+. She understood everything I was trying to say and she made my sentences clear. She'll do that with this book, too, as soon as I'm done putting it all together. But knowing I needed her wasn't enough. I couldn't afford to pay her since she wasn't running a free editing business (and rightfully so).

Literally seconds after I told her I needed her for my book yet not knowing where the money would come from, I got an email from one of my coaching clients who was purchasing more coaching, like a few months' worth, which she paid upfront in full. Seriously! Just like that, with one step out in faith that God would provide if it were His will, I had the down payment I needed to start the book editing process. Now, almost four years later and working on this third book, I'm trusting Him to come through again so this book can get into the hands of women just like you—women who need to know they are loved, accepted, and anointed for a greater purpose.

I had a similar experience when it was time to create my first book's cover. God provided there too. There were bumps along the way and the path wasn't perfect. I took a few missteps and trusted the wrong people, but my team and I saw God's hand on the project the entire time. It was truly an amazing experience to see God work out all the details. And now, more than three years later, that book has sold over 1,500 copies worldwide with very little promotion by me.

I've seen this same sort of thing happen over and over again since my divorce. I was not planning for God to elevate my ministry or anything I'm doing, nor was I trying to manipulate God into giving me my way or create something outside of His will. I'm hopeful but very realistic (my personality type) that things might not work out, even if I'm fairly sure God gave me this vision or I feel it's God's will for me to do this. I might have to wait or scrap the entire project if it doesn't work, but I'm just here trusting God to work things out for His good. Even now I see God's providence paving the way and going before me. He's still setting up the details and putting people and resources in place before I need them. He is also providing the money I'll need to fully publish this book. I'm writing chapters of this book and He's writing chapters of my life and my purpose. No amount of work on my part will make any of this perfect, but God will use it all for good—His good, His divine purpose—through His divine power. I feel it when I read back portions of what I've written and wonder, *Where did that come from? I didn't write that! That must have been something divine.*

There are so many biblical stories of ladies of fearless faith and a divine purpose. Hagar was provided for right when she needed it. Rahab was protected from harm through her faith. Ruth and Naomi had no idea what was up ahead in Bethlehem, but God didn't disappoint. Instead, He created something amazing that Ruth and Naomi got to watch unfold before their very eyes. Ruth and Hannah both desired that life be different than what they were experiencing, and God eventually came through. They got their redemption story after a huge struggle and a long wait on God, which was so worth it all in the end. But it is very hard to remember His faithfulness when I'm in that waiting period, struggling with my expectations of what I know God can and should do. He promises redemption in His Word. I know that whatever God has planned for me on this journey, any financial struggle I have will be worked out and bring Him glory. The only explanation for my success will be God because without Him, this book, my other books, and my ministry would not be possible.

Going Deeper

READ 2 CORINTHIANS 4 AND 2 PETER 1. DOES ANYTHING STAND OUT?

Write 2 Peter 1:3.

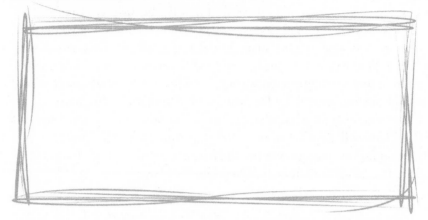

Divine: "Of or belonging to God; Appropriated to God or celebrating his praise; Pertaining to or proceeding from God; Godlike, heavenly, excellent in the highest degree, supremely admirable."[45]

Synonyms

Eternal, glorious, holy, mystical, seraphic, supernatural

How have I seen God working things out, even when I thought there was no way?

Do I believe in divine destiny and God's supernatural power to make things happen for good, even if I'm in a waiting period for my circumstances to change or get better?

Biblically Speaking

The word "divine" speaks of the attributes of God; it means "about and emanating from God." It is His character of goodness, lovingkindness, and faithfulness that flows to all of His creation. Divine is the connection between God's power and your Christian blessing. It is what you can expect when you depend on and wait on Him to accomplish His promises. Through this journey of healing, self-discovery, spiritual growth, and faith, you may think you're missing something. That you don't have everything you need and possibly God has rejected you. But that is just not God's nature. And the devil doesn't want you to see God's hands working in your life; he only wants to distract you.

Paul knows God is the One giving him the ministry of bringing the truth about Jesus to the world, as he shares in 2 Corinthians 4 because it's not a position he deserved. It's through God's mercy; it was His plan and purpose. Paul is just living with a God-conscience, *coram Deo*, in the sight of God. And he has seen the evidence of the power, God's power, at work in him, which he is sharing with the people of Corinth. God's wonderful support is available to them and everyone, just as He's given it to Paul. "The Spirit himself testifies with our spirit that we are God's children" (Romans 8:16).

Paul has fellowship with the Holy Spirit, which encourages his spiritual growth over time. He is communicating with God, who is giving him divine guidance. Paul has become a sharer in God's divine nature. He is using his anointing. Accepting this anointing and trusting in God's power fully equips him to make the journey and do the work required of him. He may be persecuted by others, friends, or family, but God will never leave. Faith helps him to stay the course.

The apostle Peter said something similar (in 2 Peter 1). He was moved by the Holy Spirit and fully equipped by God. He'd been given all he needed but it required no effort—he didn't earn it, he wasn't born with it, and it was not inherited due to anything good his family had done. It was only through knowing God that he came into the power and divine nature of

God. He knew serving Christ with his life was the highest honor, the foundation of spiritual blessings. A truly divine spiritual life is more precious than gold; it has infinite value.

> I pray that the eyes of your heart may be enlightened so that you may know the hope to which he has called you, the riches of his glorious inheritance in his holy people, and his incomparably great power for us who believe. That power is the same as the mighty strength he exerted when he raised Christ from the dead and seated him at his right hand in the heavenly realms, far above all rule and authority, power and dominion, and every name that is invoked, not only in the present age but also in the one to come. (Ephesians 1:18–21)

ABRAHAM'S JOURNEY

In Genesis 22, God gave Abraham the sacrificial ram at the very last second before he sacrificed his son Isaac. God didn't provide it when Abraham cut the burnt offering wood, when they loaded up the donkey, when they were climbing up the mountain, and not when he was laying his son in place. At that point, you'd think God wasn't going to come through or keep His promise. But His nature! He provided and kept His promises. The reason for this testing was so Abraham would demonstrate that he trusted God completely and was willing to release anything or anyone, even someone he loved (Matthew 10:37). Abraham placed God above all and proved it. At that moment, the Lord knew He was divinely connected to Abraham; there was no division in his heart.

Abraham, although not perfect, was a productive and effective servant. He was given divine directions and guidance, and he followed through on the task, trusting God would not let him down. This act was yet another confirmation that solidified their relationship based on faith. These types of manifestations, where God comes through for you at just the right time, are reminders His nature can be trusted. You can walk in confidence that His divine power is available for you too.

You have the power to stand up against the devil and label his deception as a distraction while you're waiting on God to divinely work things out. God is like the snowplow on a dark and snowy night, clearing the way so that things are clear for you in the morning. He knows what's up ahead, and when He sees obstacles, He might slow you down or detour you while He works out the details. The sovereignty of God is palpable—noticeable when you open your eyes to see.

When you want to give up, God never gets exhausted by the work it takes to make things right for His good. Everything is all right once it's done. No purpose is stopped. Through trust in Him and His timing, doors will be opened for you and miracles will happen. You will meet some amazing people of God who will guide you along the way, helping you with your purpose. You just have to be open to it, be humble, and accept these gifts. There will be divine compensation for doing His will as well. Remember, He wants to give you the desires of your heart in addition to providing for your every need.

When you know God, you know peace. God wants His children to be more like Him, to have His character, to trust Him, and to see the goodness He has to offer. Blessings flow from His goodness, giving all you need for salvation, and to bring glory to Him through your divine purpose. But you must be open to the blessing He is waiting to bestow upon you, even if it comes through someone else's hands. He's not waiting for you to tell Him what you want. He's waiting for you to release everything you want so He can give you all you need and more. He knows so much more than you know about what you need and want in this world. This is His divine providence and divine compensation.

Week 8
What's Next? What Is My Purpose?

THEREFORE, MY DEAR FRIENDS, AS YOU
HAVE ALWAYS OBEYED—NOT ONLY IN
MY PRESENCE BUT NOW MUCH MORE IN
MY ABSENCE—CONTINUE TO WORK OUT
YOUR SALVATION WITH FEAR AND
TREMBLING, FOR IT IS GOD WHO WORKS
IN YOU TO WILL AND TO ACT TO FULFILL
HIS GOOD PURPOSE.
—PHILIPPIANS 2:12–13

I'm Called to Get Well

I grew up in a stressful home with a mother who worked in administration at a local hospital. During my childhood, I experienced a lot of stomachaches and migraines. If there was any stress in my outside environment, I internalized it. There was always drama; someone was always talking behind the backs of other family members. And someone was always mad at me for something. They were very hard to be around, but they were family; putting up with each other was what we're supposed to do. It was my normal, and what I married into, until I could not take it any longer. The internalizing of the stress and the drama of other people's lives was starting to kill me.

That same month I found out I have systemic lupus erythematosus (lupus for short). I told my (now ex-) husband that I couldn't stay on the emotional roller coaster that was our marriage any longer. For a few weeks, I grieved the idea that not only was I sick with this unknown (to me) illness, but also that no matter if I stayed married or divorced, no one was going to physically take care of me. Being taken care of had never happened in my childhood or my married life. I was the caretaker and the giver, and everyone else was a taker. I felt like my life was heading down a path of destruction. I was a victim of my illness and of the adultery and pathological self-absorption that ruined my marriage.

When I went to the doctor, she seemed to be preparing me for the worst, talking about my needing disability, a handicapped parking plate, and a lot of medication. Because there is no cure for lupus, she just wanted to make me comfortable and alleviate my symptoms. For a short time, I didn't have the emotional strength to speak up. I allowed her to direct my path and prescribe a boatload of medications, all while I was being blown around in the family court. Getting well and being well was not on my radar. I was merely surviving each day, ending it in tears of hopelessness and heartache, which resulted in even more physical pain.

Toward the end of my divorce, I realized I was being taken over by everyone around me. My lawyer, doctors, and even friends were trying to help, but I was allowing them to decide and prescribe my future. I didn't want to get healthy enough to stop being a victim and take over my own life. I was allowing everyone else to be my "secondary abuser," even if that wasn't their intention. I chose to let them make all my decisions.

It was when I read the final divorce papers, prepared with information I'd never agreed to disclose, with numbers I knew were unfair and not even close to what was agreed upon, I had to get up and walk. I had to speak up! I would have preferred to stay curled up in a ball, hide in the corner, pretend none of this was happening, and hope it would all work out on its own. But I felt the push from God saying, "You need to speak up for yourself, your children, and your future. No one else is going to do this for you. I gave you a voice. Use it! I have prepared the way and I will go with you in strength; speak up, My child. Now is the time."

I took myself out of victim mode, revived myself, and internally said, *Never again.* This was the start of my healing journey. I knew I needed to get emotionally healthy for myself, set boundaries on my own life for my emotional health, be a better example for my children, and make all my own decisions. This was *my* life. I was walking with God, and He would help me make the best decisions for my future. He had an anointed purpose for my life, and letting others decide could cause me to walk away from that calling. It was a new dawn, a new chapter, and I was stepping into it scared and nervous, but it was what I needed to do.

I had to have faith God would direct me to where I needed to go and as to how certain decisions should be made. Spiritually, I needed to trust God more so I could rely less on others telling me what to do. And even if I made decisions that didn't seem to be right at first, or others questioned my reasoning, I needed to trust God would work it all out for good. He promises I need to just trust and believe, always, in all circumstances. God wants me to prosper in health and life, not merely survive and follow what the world prescribes. In working on my spiritual and emotional health, my physical health has improved. I've taken control of which drugs and supplements I put into my body, and I speak up when something is just not right.

Ladies, we need to look after our health and be the first responder anytime we sense something is physically off. No one else is going to do that work for us.

Going Deeper

READ JOHN 5:1–15. DOES ANYTHING STAND OUT?

WRITE ISAIAH 57:15.

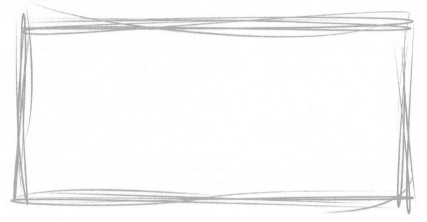

REVIVE: "To start to grow, develop, or become successful again, or to make something do this."[46]

SYNONYMS

Awaken, energize, overcome, rejuvenate, resurrect, strengthen

AM I STILL WALKING AS A VICTIM TO MY CIRCUMSTANCES OR AM I WALKING SECURELY IN MY HEALING JOURNEY?

IN WHAT WAYS CAN I ALLOW THE HOLY SPIRIT TO REVIVE MY EMOTIONAL, PHYSICAL, AND SPIRITUAL HEALTH?

Biblically Speaking

Jesus met a man at Bethesda who was paralyzed (John 5). He had been in this condition for thirty-eight years, and he was at the pool of Bethesda because the water was known to have healing powers and he needed a miracle. He was so badly disabled that he needed to be carried to this location every feast day because he couldn't walk there himself. It is doubtful he could even care for himself. "Bethesda" is Hebrew for "house of mercy." The belief was that during the Passover season or other feast seasons, an angel would come down and stir up the water and those who stepped in at that very moment were miraculously made well. Many sick, blind, lame, paralyzed, and others would wait for the water to move and jump in; but only the first in, or a favored few, received healing.

Since the paralyzed man could not move on his own, he'd never made it in in time. When the water moved, it seems like he didn't even try to crawl to the pool anymore. Maybe he did during the first few years of his condition, but as bad as his life was on those days, he was familiar with his condition. Anything different would have been unknown. He was so discouraged, he had lost his faith and fallen into victim mode. In addition, being healed would have meant the man would lose the sympathy and free welfare he received from others. Perhaps he wasn't even sure he wanted to be healed anymore.

Yet Jesus asked him, "Do you want to get well?" (v. 6). He wanted to stir up hope and build faith back into the life of this man. The man started to tell Jesus all the reasons why he couldn't move forward into healing, but Jesus wasn't bothered by his list of obstacles and instead "said to him, 'Get up; pick up your pallet and walk.' Immediately the man was healed and recovered his strength, and picked up his pallet and walked" (v. 8). Through Jesus, he was revived and given new hope and a new mindset. He got up and walked, thus able to take a different path and take care of his own life instead of depending on others to do it for him. He could go on to thrive in life.

> He asked him, Wilt thou be made whole? A strange question to be asked one that had been so long ill. Some indeed would not be made whole, because their sores serve them to beg by and serve them for an excuse for idleness; but this poor man was as unable to go a begging as to work, yet Christ put it to him, (1.) To express his own pity and concern for him. Christ is tenderly inquisitive concerning the desires of those that are in affliction, and is willing to know what is their petition: "What shall I do for you?" (2.) To try him whether he would be beholden for a cure to him against whom the great people were so prejudiced and sought to prejudice others. (3.) To teach him to value the mercy, and to excite in him desires after it. In spiritual cases, people are not willing to be cured of their sins, are loth to part with them. If this point therefore were but gained, if people were willing to be made whole, the work were half done, for Christ is willing to heal, if we be but willing to be healed. (Matthew Henry, *Matthew Henry Commentary on the Whole Bible,* 1981)

The feeling of being paralyzed, unable to move, or unable to make wise decisions can stop anyone from proceeding to faith and healing. The Greek word *anazao,* pronounced ä-nä-zä'-o, means "to revive, recover life, or regain strength." *Re-* and *vivere* mean "to live again." To revive is to awake or rejuvenate your life again after death. Because divorce feels like a death in so many ways, many women stay stuck in the surviving part of this season, unable to move forward into recovery or restoration and unwilling to hope they can flourish after divorce. Either they think they don't deserve it or that they cannot do it alone. It can be scary to think about the unknown, and it might feel safer to stay with the familiar, but the Lord is with you every step of the way. He wants you to get up and walk out of your hopelessness and despair, to "get up; pick up your pallet and walk".

The other sick people at the pool that day missed Jesus because they were so focused on waiting for the water to move, thinking there was only one way for them to heal. They didn't seek out other ways to heal. They didn't want to do the work it might take to get well. It was easier to sit by a pool and wait. Jesus is showing you a different way. He wants to revive your faith, get you out of victim mode, and put you back on a stable walking surface. The paralyzed man responded in faith and obeyed Jesus's command to walk. He was not healed in the pool but by walking with Jesus.

God is holy and able to revive the spirit of the humble, comfort people amidst their afflictions and troubles of all kinds, and heal the hearts of the broken and hurting. He has mercy for you and whatever it is you are going through. You can focus on the obstacles and find excuses that keep you stuck or you can take responsibility, stand up, and walk toward healing and freedom. Jesus died, rose again, and was revived. He did not lie dormant after a time of healing and preparation. Freshen yourself for the journey ahead. Heal your soul and your body, which is the temple of God's presence.

"Dear friend, I pray that you may enjoy good health and that all may go well with you, even as your soul is getting along well" (3 John 1:2) is a prayer for you to prosper, not in material wealth but good health. Your body is only here temporarily, but your soul will last forever. God calls you to live again after a divorce. Now is the time to revive your soul—mind, will, and emotions—and your physical body. It's time to recover, to live again, to building your prosperous future. Your spiritual, emotional, and physical health is worth the work in this restoration journey, and God will be your helper in it all.

I'm Called to Comfort Others

When I was in high school, I was invited to join a peer-led school support group. A licensed family counselor instructed the group to support and mentor other teenagers through difficult circumstances. We'd meet with the counselor, share our own personal or family issues, encourage one another in the group, and then comfort other students or guide them to seek adult assistance, as per our training. I'm still not sure why I didn't see this as my calling or at least my career path at the time, because I enjoyed it so much. The instructor let me know I was a natural at encouraging and comforting others but warned me that a degree in psychology was pretty much useless without a master's degree. But instead of social work, as she suggested, I continued at community college majoring in accounting.

That career path came to an abrupt end when I failed Accounting 101. That, too, should have been the sign to go back and look at what I'd been good at, but I decided to try the medical field next. Honestly, I was just looking for a job rather than a purpose. I didn't know I needed a purpose. I was taught that a career after college was a necessity for the sole purpose of making a lot of money so I could be successful in life. This was not great advice for me, and it's not what I've told my children to do with their lives. Fulfilling a purpose doesn't always require a college education. Going to college just for the sake of getting a degree so as to make more money is the wrong path for most people; instead, we should seek God to direct our path and to light the way, and we can expect divine compensation for doing what He says.

Being a writer and coach and running a ministry don't require a college education. God has found other ways to equip and prepare me for this purpose in the form of spiritual gifts and life experiences. I don't regret my college degrees because I gained a lot from those classes and from my instructors, but I regret the reasons for going and the consequences of student loan debt. Don't feel that you need to go back to school to do well. Figure out what you're here for first and choose your strategy second. You'll find your niche in life a lot faster that way.[47]

Comforting others is part of my purpose. I may have not known God during my high school years, but I could accept His healing by connecting with other teens who were going through the same things I was. Shared trauma is a bond all of us can understand. I accepted comfort and gave comfort all at the same time. Knowing others who felt my pain and suffering was comforting. Learning to share my struggles with others not only released any shame that held me back but also helped me feel (what I now know is) God's comfort.

Through many trials and errors, I've learned that not only do I have a gift of empathy along with encouragement and support, but also that God uses all of my gifts to do what He has designed me to do. And although I've done many things to earn money, and I am willing to do whatever I can in the future, God is the ultimate provider. If He gives me a plan and a purpose, He will provide the income to support that purpose. All I have to do is trust and obey.

Knowing my writing and encouragement help someone get through another day, with whatever they are facing, brings me comfort and gets me through my own tough days. It reminds me that nothing I have faced was in vain, and I get the reminder I was created for this exact purpose. I was called to comfort. Find out what were you called to do and you'll start feeling alive again.

Going Deeper

READ 2 CORINTHIANS 1. DOES ANYTHING STAND OUT?

WRITE 2 CORINTHIANS 1:4.

COMFORT: "A state of physical ease and freedom from pain or constraint."[48]

SYNONYMS

Compassion, consolation, encouragement, relief, solace, support

IN WHAT WAYS CAN GOD USE WHAT I'VE BEEN THROUGH TO HELP OTHERS?

IS HE CALLING ME TO REACH OUT TO SOMEONE IN NEED OF COMFORT AND ENCOURAGEMENT?

Biblically Speaking

There is joy in knowing "the God of all comfort" (2 Corinthians 1:3–4). The Greek word Paul chose for "all comfort" in this verse is *paraklesis,* pronounced par-ak'-lay-sis, meaning a "calling or summons for help." It's a soothing sympathy, a strengthening, making you strong and brave. God gives you the Holy Spirit to be your *paraclete,* pronounced par-uh-kleet. He is your advocate and comforter, staying close to your heart and sharing God's gift of grace and mercy.

When you cry out to God for comfort, He is close and ready to soothe your soul and strengthen you so you can endure the long trials. When you take a pain pill for a headache, you are only guaranteed a few hours of relief, but comfort from God can last much, much longer. God is an inextinguishable spring that supplies comfort when no one else can. Humans are fallible and will let you down. God never does. He never walks out and never tires of the work of comforting His children. You may have been brought low by your circumstances, but the Paraclete brings you back from near death. You can appreciate the highs because you've experienced the lows. You also know you can trust God to bring you back up out of the darkness and into the light because He has always done so.

You can feel His presence in the spiritual realm, especially when you need Him the most. He is always with you, even if you cannot see Him. Sometimes you'll feel His spirit, His lovingkindness, like a weighted blanket around you; or you'll experience His presence in the form of other people who have been through the same struggles you have—to support you and bring you His comfort.

God wants you to receive His blessed comfort. He wants to calm the raging fears of your soul. He says, "Let your heart not be troubled, nor let it be afraid. [Let My perfect peace calm you in every circumstance and give you courage and strength for every challenge.]" (John 14:1 AMP). He wants to deliver you out of your pain and suffering. His comfort is not to make you cheerful, it's to soothe your fears and fill you with His peace so you can live life on purpose rather than in pain. God comforts you while you are going through your divorce, and you can comfort others in the future. Comfort is a two-step process of receiving and giving: First you reveal your hurts and needs to others, allowing them to bring you comfort and acceptance. You accept that gift from God, brought to you through His children. Then you share that same gift with those who reveal their distress to you. The souls connect through their shared trauma, and the healing process begins.

Empathetic and understanding people are comforters to the world. These types of people not only provide comfort; they also provide their physical presence, a listening ear, and a suggestion or two when someone needs advice. This is especially helpful for women who verbally process their way through pain and grief. Often, a hurting person just needs someone to fill in the physical gap between her and the Spirit, and as a fellow follower of Jesus, you are meant to "encourage one another and build each other up, just as in fact you are doing" (1 Thessalonians 5:11). We all need it, no matter what we are discouraged about.

Knowing God's comfort for yourself motivates you to encourage and edify others. Instead of being discouraged by world events or circumstances, you know better days are coming, that the pits of despair you fall into never last forever. (I've been where you are.) God will get you through, just as He's done for others before you. I want you to know this truth in your bones. I want you to "know [practically, through personal experience] the love of Christ which far surpasses [mere] knowledge [without experience], that you may be filled up [throughout your being] to all the fullness of God [so that you may have the richest experience of God's presence in your lives, completely filled and flooded with God Himself]" (Ephesians 3:9 AMP). You will be better equipped to serve Him and fulfill your divine purpose in the time you have left so you can look back on your life and see all the people you blessed. Comforting others is something we can all do more of.

> Suffering in another human being is a call to the rest of us to stand in community. It is a call to be there. Suffering is not a question which demands an answer, it is not a problem which requires a solution, it is a mystery which demands a presence. (John Wyatt, *Matters of Life and Death*)

I'm Called to Be Salt and Light

As a married woman, I always thought I was supposed to be super sweet; yet I was often silently judgmental and legalistic. I thought Christian women were always supposed to be serving others without complaint, never supposed to speak up or stand up for anything, and especially not minister to anyone other than their children. After my divorce, I dove deep into learning what a "Christian" woman was supposed to look like because the passive, resentful, and legalistic woman I had become didn't seem to fit. Being that way was causing me more stress; I was feeling less peace.

The first story I read in the *Boundaries* book, by Drs Henry Cloud and John Townsend, resonated with me because I was in similar types of relationships with people. I would give and give until I was empty inside with nothing left to give. Then I'd be angry and resentful toward the people closest to me. It was easy to say yes to everyone but myself, but I was very angry when people expected even more from me, not understanding I was overwhelmed and overdoing it.

After I had read the *Boundaries* book, I started to use my voice. I could speak up for myself, say no, and decide what was best for me and my own life as a divorced woman. I took some time to practice boundaries in all of my relationships, which didn't make everyone happy, and I decided to spend a year focusing on being my authentic self. Then, sometime later, that same counselor suggested I read Rachel Held Evan's book *The Year of Biblical Womanhood. Oh, no, no, no,* I wasn't going to read *that book.* That was the author and book my former husband saw on a television talk show and suggested I read it to learn to be a "better wife." On the show, Rachel Held Evans (RHE) was sharing how she stood at the city gate of her town holding a sign, calling her husband "lord," and telling everyone how awesome he was. My husband said he wanted me to be more like her or do more of what he thought she was doing. There was no way was I was going to read about how I was supposed to do more in my marriage when I already felt resentment for all I *was* doing, and for having nothing left to give because I wasn't getting anything in return. I was triggered.

When the New Year broke into 2016 and after being divorced for two years and working on my boundaries, authenticity, and healing, I decided I was ready to read her book. I had been hearing a lot more about Rachel Held Evans that prior year and what she believed as a Christian feminist. I figured I needed to read it for me. I needed to conquer this book that had become a trigger for me every time I heard about it. This was after reading a couple of Henry Cloud's books and *No More Christian Nice Girl* by Paul Coughlin. I felt I was ready to read whatever RHE had to say in this book, even if it was everything my ex-husband thought it was.

The book that I expected to repress me actually empowered and educated me. I didn't agree with everything she wrote, but it was exactly what I needed to hear for my growth. RHE was a light in the dark places of my heart—the parts that didn't want to be one of those "Christians" anymore. That word had become tainted in my mind by the behavior of the people in the church that shamed me and judged me. They called themselves Christians, but I didn't want to associate with people who oppressed women, were judgmental and legalistic, and expected me to be meek, passive, and free of resentment. This never felt right to me. I wasn't living in the freedom of Christ by following their rules of acceptance. RHE said that was never what Jesus meant for Christianity, and thanks to her insight and compassion, I was able to safely explore how I felt about my religion of more than twenty years.

An interesting thing happened when I announced on my Facebook and Instagram pages that I would be tackling her book. Some women said the same thing I had two years prior, and a few others scolded me for reading such a "wretched book." One woman, who also wrote about abuse online, actually implied my Christianity would be at risk if I read it. I laughed at that one—I had a degree from a Christian college and had taken many Bible study courses, and I knew how to use discernment, especially when reading a book by another fallible author. I can read, research using hermeneutics, and use discernment to help me come to my conclusion.

Side Note: I hope you've been doing the same in this book. Take what you need and ignore what you do not agree with, based on your research of biblical texts.

> I knew somewhere deep in my bones that a revolution was afoot, that the women of this earth were rising up, and that, in some way great or small, I was going to be a part of it. (Rachel Held Evans, *A Year of Biblical Womanhood*)

I felt the same way as RHE. I couldn't believe someone would judge me so harshly for just reading a book. I couldn't be part of the legalism, the criticism, and the judgment of people who said they loved God and were able to hear the Holy Spirit for themselves. I couldn't stay quiet or say to women that they must continue to endure disrespect and abuse just to preserve a marriage promise that had already been broken by the other party. I knew Christianity was not based on following a set of rules decided upon by a select few. I knew I needed to learn more about faith, grace, and God's love for those who love Him. That explorative journey has to led me to believe all I've shared with you in this book. I hope I can encourage you to take that journey with the Holy Spirit for yourself and your emotional healing.

Now I try to encourage and empower women to be women of valor, just like RHE empowered me. Women can hear the Holy Spirit and use discernment. Women can speak up and share their truth and purpose. Women can do the same work as men for the kingdom. I can speak up, even to a man, be assertive, and not allow another human to push me around or make me feel less than because I'm not male, or that because of my divorce I've "lost" that right. And most importantly, I don't have to be a sugary sweet Christian girl, waiting to be led around by a future husband. I am led every single day by what the Holy Spirit tells me to say, write, and do to live out my divine purpose.

I've become a lighthouse for those who've gone through the same rough waters I went through, blowing my horn at anyone trying to stop women from feeling they can't divorce or that it's a sin. To God be the glory for comforting me, healing my anger and bitterness, stopping me from being like other legalistic Christians, and putting me on a solid foundation. From that foundation, I can shine a light in the dark places of abuse and divorce, especially in the church.

Recently, a local pastor told me divorce was a "taboo subject." Well, that means divorced women need lots more comfort! I sent him a copy of my first book and I'll send him this one as well, in the hope that he learns we are not taboo people. We just want to be loved by God and His people and be the salt and light He has called us to be.

Going Deeper

READ MATTHEW 5:13–14. DOES ANYTHING STAND OUT?

WRITE COLOSSIANS 4:6.

SEASONED: "Mixed or sprinkled with something that gives a relish; tempered; moderated; qualified; matured."[49]

SYNONYMS

Instructed, knowledgeable, qualified, prepared, toughened, wise

AM I SEASONED WITH SALT OR SUGAR OR BOTH?

HOW HAS GOD PREPARED, QUALIFIED, AND INSTRUCTED ME TO USE MY VOICE TO SPEAK UP FOR MYSELF, FOR OTHERS, OR TO OTHERS, EVEN WHEN I FEEL SCARED?

IS MY VOICE TARNISHED BY LEGALISM IN ANY WAY?

HOW CAN I WORK ON MY EMOTIONAL HEALTH SO I'M BETTER ABLE TO LOVE AND CARE FOR MYSELF AND OTHERS?

Biblically Speaking

Paul appealed often for Christian maturity. He gave instructions about clear communication, making the most of each opportunity, and effective outreach to others in (Colossians 4). He asked the Colossians to show kindness and ongoing, unselfish love in all their relationships. Jesus taught that His people are called to be salt and light in the world (Matthew 5:13–14). Be confident in your faith, seasoned with salt, and a light shining for others to see God's glory within you rather than grounded in legalism.

Just to be clear: this includes having appropriate boundaries. Boundaries are necessary for every relationship so that each person always has autonomy. A woman can be kind and have assertive boundaries at the same time. Love can be loving, kind, *and* tough. Jesus was kind but He wasn't the "nicest" human to walk the earth. He was bold in His speech against sin and injustice, but love was always His motivation, never judgment.

> The goal when emulating the real Jesus is to become both sweet and salty, both gracious and firm. (Paul Coughlin, *No More Christian Nice Girl: When Just Being Nice, Instead of Good, Hurts You, Your Family, and Your Friends*)

WHAT DOES BEING "SALTY" MEAN?

The earliest recorded use of salt was in 2700 BC. It was used to preserve meat from decay and to bring out a better flavor. Now, salt is widely used in the chemical and beauty industries, with approximately 14,000 different uses. The salt on top of your caramel chocolate candy piece brings out the sweetness in the caramel and the bitter chocolate. It changes the flavor of what it's been added to. Just like homemade chocolate chip cookies require salt, relationships require saltiness for the same reason—to bring out your sweetness and complete the recipe. Your words either preserve or destroy the message of Christ.

Salt was also used for currency, which made it valuable. Your presence and words can bring value to any life. "Saltiness" means "to use uplifting words, edify others, and be helpful." Jesus was firm when He needed to be (overturning tables with those who knew what they were doing) but was gracious and confident in God's love when He found a woman in sin and gave her a reason to hope (John 8:6–8). Rather than punishing her with His words, He "said to her, 'Woman, where are they? Did no one condemn you?' She answered, 'No one, Lord!' And Jesus said, 'I do not condemn you either. Go. From now on sin no more.']" (vv. 10–11 AMP). Notice that rather than highlight the Law, He asked her to look around for her punishers, to notice her newfound freedom for herself. He wasn't interested in judging her past; He was interested in her living out her bold and free future.

Religious legalism is the belief that to achieve salvation and right standing with God, one must perform certain deeds, behaviors, disciplines, and practices. The Pharisees and Sadducees were the legalists of Jesus's time. They are still active today under different names. They can be found in most any church, pretending to follow Christ but instead following their own sets of rules and procedures that do not get anyone into heaven. It is only through faith that you can know God as intimately as Jesus does.

"Salt is good, but if it loses its saltiness, how can you make it salty again? Have salt among yourselves, and be at peace with each other" (Mark 9:50). Your salty, sweet words can be rooted in love and compassion, sprinkled with grace and mercy, just as Jesus's were. They can bring peace. This light is what will bring people to Jesus, not sharing a list of rules to follow. Jesus brought people to Him with words of wisdom and loving compassion, especially when others were judgmental. He didn't say, "Go ahead, throw stones at the sinner; she deserves it." Instead, He said, "Let any one of you who is without sin be the first to throw a stone at her" (John 8:7). What compassion He had for this woman with His words and His actions! Jesus showed that women had as much value as men, as much need to be treated with kindness and respect. The Pharisees wanted to harm her, yet they claimed to represent God. He wanted the woman to know His love. We're called to be Christlike, not legalistic.

Jesus lived God's message of lovingkindness with the world out loud. He became the good news of a love great enough and big enough to redeem and restore everything. The message of His life, and the message that can be yours, is that God always loves and forgives, and He never stops. You are called to share the love of the Lord with the world—even if it's just in your small corner of it.

> God likes his women with a firm will that aligns with his will. Strong, courageous women who get in line with the will of God are destined to change their corner of the world. (Paul Coughlin, *No More Christian Nice Girl*)

Jesus said Christians should stand out—not for their judgment or criticism, and not for being "better" than others, but for how peaceful and assured they are about their future (Matthew 5:13–14). The more of God's love you receive and trust, the less you are distracted by the devil's schemes to divide and destroy your harmony. You trust God more and more each day that He's holding you and He will get you through any difficulty. To the non-Christian watching, you can be a lighthouse, an oasis of peace they feel safe around; a comfort in the midst of their troubles.

"Let your conversation be always full of grace, seasoned with salt, so that you may know how to answer everyone" (Colossians 4:6). Those who want to know Jesus will have questions, and they'll feel safe asking those questions of Christians who are loving, not judgmental and unkind. Does God's love shine through you? When you're devouring the Word, remember why it tastes so good to you—because it's seasoned with salt, with an underlying sweetness of knowing you are a daughter of God, and that will never change. His Word is seasoned, and so are you for consuming it. Others will see Him in you and through you. Let that saltiness preserve the truth of God's never-ending grace and mercy in your life.

So shine your light, and don't let another human or the enemy put it out. Satan will try to convince you that you can't encourage someone else, but you can and you will, just by being who God created you to be. You're designed to be a strong, authentic, assertive, and empowered woman who's ready to take action when God gives the call, not a "nicey, nicey" passive Christian woman with no voice. Many people are waiting to taste and see that the Lord is good. Preserve yourself with salt so you can be exactly what they need. Get into that lighthouse and start spreading His light over the rocks to light up their safe passage home.

I'm Called to Take Action

I was very nervous when I first started blogging about my divorce. I felt that I'd be shamed or that people would think I wasn't a good enough wife to keep my husband (the topic of many of my blog articles). I also didn't trust my ability to write or speak eloquently enough to be a writer or public speaker. My homeschool blog was filled with curriculum reviews, pictures of our field trips, and an occasional learning lesson—nothing like all the writing I do now. I went from teaching my children to encouraging and teaching divorcing and divorced women. Sometimes I'm still not sure I'm completely ready to do this work God has called me to do, but I do it anyway. I do it scared and feeling unprepared.

In late 2016, I felt led to start my YouTube channel, talking about abuse and divorce recovery. For many months, I was able to talk myself out of recording a video (I still do). I was able to record my first video and started to edit out all the *uhs* and *umms*. Realizing just how bad it was, I deleted it. I deleted several after that as well, telling God I couldn't talk right, even with a script. I was good at criticizing myself. *But I kept trying.* With each unpublished video, as well as the first videos, I practiced as the Holy Spirit guided me. Slowly they started getting better—enough so that one of my videos had over 64,000 views by the end of 2020. Those first videos were horrible, in my opinion. But when I realized they helped someone, lots of someones, I knew I had done something right. My job was not to please myself, or even those who were expecting videos made by a production team. My job is to do what God has asked me to do, and that's exactly what those first videos are still doing.

If I had waited until I could do everything perfectly, I would still not have started. I had to learn as I went, trusting God to open doors and to teach me what I needed to learn as I continued to take action. The same could be said about my writing. Writing blog posts, books, and even freelance pieces all take loads of practice to become articles millions want to read, but I had to start somewhere. I had to trust Him that someone needed those first articles and videos just at that time. They couldn't wait for me to "get perfect" at it. They just needed to know they weren't alone right in their moment of need.

I had to wait when God said to wait, learn what I needed to learn, take action when there was an opportunity, and sometimes wait again for things to happen. It has not been one opportunity and door opening after another. When doors are closed, I trust Him and listen for the call to move when they are opened. Being used by God and answering His call is a lot like work. A lot of days it is just work, work, and more work while not seeing much action or any rewards; and other days I just rest or do another "job" He has me to doing in that season. I've completed (almost) three books, all on the instructions from God to take action and ignore my need for things to look perfect. I've written articles for large Christian websites with millions of readers. I've created over eighty videos that have over 200,000 views. I've spoken to a room of thirty mothers of preschoolers. I did all these things because God told me to do good work and keep on doing it. He has never told me to stop, so I just keep going and pushing forward.

Even when I serve one woman and she says, "I needed that exact thing you are saying right now," it makes all the days of hard work and struggle, as well as the days of doing something else, worth it. That appreciation for my being God's representative, His hands, and feet here on earth, encourages me to keep doing what I was created for. I'm merely a vessel. I'm nothing special. I have no special talent. But God made me for this, just as He made you for many reasons too. Doing this gives my life meaning and purpose, and when people verbalize their appreciation of it, my heart fills with joy that can I hold on to during the mundane days.

As of today, my first book has sold about 1,500 copies. That's too few for big publishing houses; they would've stopped printing more of my books because they need huge numbers to keep a book going. But to me, knowing 1,500 women have a copy of that book and it has helped them feel like they, too, can survive their divorce, keeps me going. It's proof I've done a good work I should never stop doing. To me, sales are people helped, not products sold or money made. They are taking control of their restoration journey, as God has called them to do. I have the same hope for this book. If I can bring at least one woman back to her faith and back to the place of peace only Jesus provides (John 14:27), and she goes on to bless others who then bless others, then my life is on track with God's plan for me. I don't need to personally serve millions because I can do so just by serving one or a few. We all are given power through the Holy Spirit to fulfill our purpose, and for most of us we'll accomplish everything we're meant to through our trust, our determination to live in and through Him, and our willingness to keep going. I'm in the service business. My job is to serve the Lord, do His work, and stop for no one.

As previously stated, I have my days of struggle. I repeat that often so you understand that no woman's path is easy, no matter how easy she makes it look. Some people try to stop me from doing my work for whatever reason, which causes me to think I should stop. Some days I am hit with a massive diversion and get very frustrated. On the tough days, when I want to give up and find another line of work because I think it would be easier, I remind myself I'd only be letting evil win. My declaration is then: *I'm doing a great work and I'm not coming down!*

Join me. Find your purpose, live it, and don't let anyone or anything drag you away from being who you are meant to be. Live your life fully "in" it.

Going Deeper

READ NEHEMIAH 2, 4, AND 6. DOES ANYTHING STAND OUT?

WRITE 1 CORINTHIANS 15:58.

LABOR: "Work, especially hard physical work; making great effort; have difficulty in doing something despite working hard."[50]

SYNONYMS

Advancement, diligence, effort, endeavor, exertion, undertaking

HOW IS GOD ADVANCING ME TOWARD MY DIVINE PURPOSE?

WHAT WORK IS HE IS ASKING ME TO DO?

WHAT ARE THE THINGS, OR WHO ARE THE PEOPLE, THAT DISTRACT ME OR KEEP ME FROM DOING WHAT GOD HAS CALLED ME TO DO?

HOW CAN I STAY FOCUSED ON THE TASKS OR JOB HE NEEDS ME TO DO?

Biblically Speaking

The word "advance" has several meanings. As you move forward in the healing journey, the biblical meaning of "advance" is "progressing forward, advancing to a higher rank, accelerating growth." As you become increasingly dependent on God's strength, He will promote you to a higher level. He calls you to take action to advance while He arranges everything to empower your move forward. It's a synergy—both you needing God and Him needing you to accomplish the goal.

The goal is to fulfill your purpose; the actions are the steps He wants you to take to get there. He has prepared you for this hard work and He will be with you in the struggle and the labor. No matter your profession, job position, age, or level of ability, you have a God-given, divine destiny. He wants you to use the gifts He has given you to fulfill His purpose (your purpose) through your life. Your work with God needs your participation. Only you can do it. Are you willing to take action, even if it means life might get harder and forces might try to trouble you and make you stop?

Work for the Lord, no matter how you think people value your work. Grow the fruit of the Spirit and take action to share that fruit with others. Find joy in the job you have, no matter how small. Everything has its season and God will not waste a learning opportunity. Find joy in each part of your journey. And never let anyone tell you you should not be doing the task God has for you or the work you delight in.

NEHEMIAH: FACING THE OPPOSITION

When you read through chapter 2 of Nehemiah, you get a behind-the-scenes look at what taking action looks like. Nehemiah was a cupbearer, serving God by serving the king and doing his job as faithfully as he knew how while feeling a strong desire to do something bigger. He was in preparation and waiting mode. He waited and prayed in anticipation for four months for the right time to do something. Nehemiah trusted God and let Him lead. He had God's backing. The king, his current boss, noticed his downcast mood and asked him about it. The door was opened to take action, to make his request. Nehemiah was dreadfully afraid but he spoke anyway; he was honest and authentic instead of hiding. Nehemiah shared on what he felt was right and what he was led to do—rebuild Jerusalem's wall. What happened next was amazing—God's divine provision. God worked everything out for good. The hand of God was all over this work He wanted done, and overnight, Nehemiah was free to begin his work.

> The work of God requires stamina. Nehemiah sustained his stamina even through staggering difficulties. Nehemiah's willingness to be personally involved in the work, as well as his ability to convey the need to others, resulted in a task force that completed this enormous building project in a mere fifty-two days—to the glory of God. Like any godly leader, Nehemiah did not go unchallenged. Yet, he sustained his stamina in the face of every opposition. (Paul Chappell, *Leaders Who Make a Difference*)

When God asks anyone to do good work, the opposition's ears perk up, listening and anticipating where it can prevent or delay this effort. Your opposition doesn't want you to be productive in your work or divine tasks. The opposition wants you to fail or quit before you even start. Nehemiah experienced that very thing when he was working on the wall. His response was to pray. God raised him, literally and figuratively, every time he was met with resistance, yet he didn't succumb to the pressure. Instead, he gave it all to God.

Sanballat and Tobiah (Nehemiah's opposition) hated the Jewish people and Nehemiah. First they sent a letter telling him to stop. Then they laughed at him. They even used his friends to try to scare him. Nehemiah did his best to just ignore them as he continued his work. Nehemiah's divine responsibility could not be hindered by the crowd's taunting. Their mockery didn't even deserve a response.

The opposition started attacking Nehemiah and the other laborers to get them to stop the work they were doing. But instead of quitting, Nehemiah kept facing this opposition objectively and justly. He found ways to fight the opposition and continue his work at the very same time. And when they tried to get him to come down from where he was building on the wall, he said, "I am carrying on a great project and cannot go down. Why should the work stop while I leave it and go down to you?" His enemies asked him four times, and each time this was his same answer! He would not just quit to even meet with the toxic people whose only purpose was to stop him from doing what God called him to do.

This angered Nehemiah's enemies even more, as it usually does when God has promoted people to a higher purpose and they are laboring for the Lord.

GIVE YOURSELF FULLY FOR THE WORK OF THE LORD

"My dear brothers and sisters, stand firm. Let nothing move you. Always give yourselves fully to the work of the Lord, because you know that your labor in the Lord is not in vain" (1 Corinthians 15:58 NIV). Be steadfast and anchored in Him. God has a great supply of all you need. He has abundant resources, enabling you to abound in strength when you stay deeply rooted in Him. "I pray that out of his glorious riches he may strengthen you with power through his Spirit in your inner being" (Ephesians 3:16).

God has established you, as He did Nehemiah, and will advance you to a higher place. God will give you your divine direction and sustain you for the labor. You can be confident in that. Nothing you do for the Lord is done in vain. Be diligent in your effort and you'll be successful in your endeavor as you continue your work. Refuse to come down for anyone until the great work is done.

I'm Called to Thrive

After I started working on creating healthy boundaries with the people in my new life after divorce, I wanted to know how to thrive. I was tired of just surviving and getting through each day. Life seemed to be about putting out one fire after another. I had gotten so used to living this way, I was always expecting the next bad thing to happen. This caused anxiety and fear, as I was never prepared for life alone.

Many of my coaching clients have asked me, "How do you thrive after divorce? What does thriving look like? What are my assertive rights as a human being?" For me, these were not things I was taught growing up. I needed to surround myself with emotionally healthy, thriving people—a hard group of people to find. I needed to know what they looked like and how they behaved. I was raised in a toxic home and needed "normals" in my life to figure it out. As I met new people and got to know some of my long-term friends better (there is more time for that after divorce), I started to notice something about thriving people: they don't worry about what's going to happen next. They don't ruminate on what has happened either. They don't remind themselves of their struggles or chew on how they deserved it. Instead, they know the hope of the future—the hope that everything will work out. And they plan for the good things while having a backup plan for the troubles that are usually inevitable. They know what God has in store for them—everything worked out for good. Whoa!

I have to keep reminding myself this world is not my home. No matter what happens, no matter how bad something looks, God is going to take care of it. In the end, all will be fine. Life is about always keeping God's long-term plans in mind. It's thinking of this difficulty, *What I'm facing is nothing in the grand scheme of eternity. Thousands and thousands of years from now, if I'm able to reflect on my life here on earth, is this one thing going to matter? Probably not! It will be all worked out. It will probably make me stronger, and I may even be glad it happened*—that's how I feel about my divorce now.

When I've passed on and think back to my time on earth, I want to know I was doing my very best to be full of the fruit of the Spirit (Galatians 5:22–23). I know heaven will be way better than here but I don't want to remember an entirely miserable life. Certain aspects make me sad, some bittersweet, but I want to live life in abundance, with a promise of an afterlife. This helps to keep a smile on my face and patience in my heart.

One song that always comes to mind and seems to remind me of what having faith and thriving means is Ryan Stevenson's "Amadeo (Still My God)." He sings of how God is always our rock and our hope, no matter what kind of pain or tragedy we experience. He is our unchanging Father of love, hope, joy, peace, and strength. He is all we need. No matter what we've experienced when going through a painful divorce and what I've been writing about in this book, God is still our God, still our hope, still our peace and joy. We just have to still believe.

Mr. Stevenson has this to say about this song on his website, ryanstevensonmusic.com:

> Amadeo is derived from the Latin name Amadeus which means 'lover of God.' We live in an uncertain world, and the truth of our humanity is the fact that we will all face uncertainties in life. Uncertainties can sometimes be catastrophic, life-altering events, that shake the foundations of our faith and can leave us disillusioned. My prayer for this song is to encourage all of us, to trust God no matter what our circumstances may be, to remind us that whether in crisis or victory, our first response should always be to cry out to the Lord! In the midst of trials and storms, may we all be able to hold steadfast to the Lord, our comforter and peace, and

always be able to say, "I trust You, God, I love You, God! In every valley or mountain top, You are still my God!"

Being practical now: How do I thrive? I am deeply planted in the house of the Lord. I believe in His promises because I know I belong to Him and that He wants me to bloom and flourish. I get my strength to continue to walk this path from the Spirit within me. I'm flourishing after the devastation of divorce while being an almost-empty nester, getting up well into middle age, and living without a life partner. I find peace in comforting and contributing to the well-being of others. And even through writing this book, I've learned right along with you, walking the same path to rebuilding my faith and trusting Him in the journey. I feel God's love radiate through His words. Everything I've written has come from Him, not from anything I already knew. I research, trust, listen, and obey. Was it always easy? Nope, but if you're reading this, you'll know I made it through and will continue my faith journey.

I will continue to flourish through the hope I am deeply rooted in—that this world is not my home and things will get better, and if not here on earth then in heaven. I live in full surrender to God's personal growth plan because I love God and He loves me, not because I need to for my salvation. I am full of joy that God is still God and nothing—not separation nor death nor suffering—will separate me from God's lovingkindness. These deep roots keep me secure no matter what. When I feel weak, I cry out to God to keep me upright. This is how I thrive. This is my hope for you as well.

The righteous will thrive like a green leaf. (Proverbs 11:28)

Going Deeper

READ PSALM 92:12–15 AND JEREMIAH 17:7–8. DOES ANYTHING STAND OUT?

WRITE OUT PSALM 52:8–9.

THRIVE: "To grow vigorously; to progress toward or realize a goal despite or because of circumstances."[51]

SYNONYMS

Bloom, develop, flourish, radiate, shine, succeed

AM I DEEPLY ROOTED SO I CAN THRIVE, NO MATTER WHAT HAPPENS IN MY LIFE?

OR AM I SURVIVING EACH DAY, MONTH, OR YEAR?

IF SOMETHING BAD HAPPENS, HOW AM I PREPARED AND HOW MUCH AM I TRUSTING GOD?

Biblically Speaking

God makes the righteous flourish. Remember, you are made righteous by the blood of Jesus Christ, not by what you did or didn't do. This means that as a woman of faith, you are meant to thrive rather than merely survive each day. You are meant for more than anxiety, worry, and struggle. You are meant to be blessed and to feel God's blessings. Those things don't happen or not happen because you aren't thriving; they still happen despite thriving. God wants you to accept your current condition, no matter what that is, and learn to flourish right where God has you planted. God sees you. He calls you to thrive. He wants you to be rooted in Him so you can stand tall during any future storms.

The cedar tree, *cedrus libani*, of Lebanon is known for its size, strength, durability, elevation, and usefulness. Its high-quality timber has been used for thousands of years. God told Moses to use the bark to treat leprosy (Leviticus 14:4). Solomon used the timbers to build the temple of Jerusalem. It's a symbol of righteousness and pride of the world. It was often used to make coffins because it could stand the test of time and decay. When you are rooted deeply like the cedar tree and planted in divine soil, He holds you in place so you can stand the test of time.

The one thing you can be sure of in this life is trouble and death. Life should be defined as "a continued training in this trouble-solving operation." You are given the task to seek God and trust Him for the solutions, especially when you cannot see. That's faith. Your mission is to find His divine soil and put down your roots for the long haul. This helps your soul to gain strength for the troubles that happen in the future; this is being planted deeply in the house of the Lord. It's a permanent residence. Nothing can separate you from this position. You are being held in place by the strongest power this world has ever known.

You have a choice to thrive each day or to see each day as another day to get through, counting down until something great happens. God would prefer you to see each day as an opportunity to bloom right where you are, deeply rooted in Him, and to shine your inner light very brightly for all to see. This is having His gladness of heart for each new day, the gladness to do it all over again for Him.

> This is what I have observed to be good: that it is appropriate for a person to eat, to drink and to find satisfaction in their toilsome labor under the sun during the few days of life God has given them—for this is their lot. Moreover, when God gives someone wealth and possessions, and the ability to enjoy them, to accept their lot and be happy in their toil—this is a gift of God. They seldom reflect on the days of their life, because God keeps them occupied with gladness of heart. (Ecclesiastes 5:18–20)

Gladness and contentment of the heart are a byproduct of a thriving life and the environment in which you are living. Thriving is about the environment and mindset, learning to be content in all circumstances. God wants you to be a plant that grows abundantly, regardless of the climate it lives in.

"I know what it is to be in need, and I know what it is to have plenty. I have learned the secret of being content in any and every situation, whether well fed or hungry, whether living in plenty or want. I can do all this through him who gives me strength" (Philippians 4:12–13). He gives you the strength to do all things, at all times. You don't grow off your effort. You grow and flourish by staying connected to the Creator of all living things. He is your nourishment, the food for your soul, the water to keep you from thirst.

> A root set in the finest soil, in the best climate, and blessed with all that sun and air and rain can do for it, is not so sure a way of its growth to perfection, as every man may be whose spirit aspires after all that which God is ready and infinitely desirous to give him. For the sun meets not the springing bud that stretches toward him with half that certainty as God, the source of all good, communicates Himself to the soul that longs to partake of Him. (Rev. William Law, *The Spirit of Prayer*)

A thriving woman perceives and interacts with the world and life as another opportunity to be her best self. It's a thriving mindset. You can have a few bad years and still thrive.

> Shut out the noise,
> feed your mind and heart,
> accept what is, and
> let go of what you cannot control.

Closely surround yourself with people who have the same type of positive, thriving attitude you desire. When you do all of this, God will cultivate your soul while you're cultivating and contributing to the well-being of others—those God has called you to minister to.

Note from Jen

God is always with you. He always has been and He always will be. You can trust Him with your heart no matter what you go through because His love is great enough and big enough to heal, redeem, and restore everything. Everything in your life can be re-spun to shine, to bless others, to make life whole. It takes an open heart, the willingness to give all shame and regrets to Jesus, and the trust to receive all the love He has to give. It takes the desire to know Him as deeply as you want and to invite Him to walk with you on the journey. (If you don't know Jesus yet, tell Him you'd like to, and invite Him in to your life and heart.)

> When you know Jesus,
> You have an open door to His heart,
> A beautiful plan for your life,
> A life free of shame,
> A purpose to live for,
> Multiple gifts to bless others with,
> God's perfect timing,
> God's strength and encouragement to "be all that,"
> And you have hope.
>
> *You shine!*

Let's shine together.

[1] Definitions.net, STANDS4 LLC, 2021. Definition of *"presence."* Accessed January 14, 2021. https://www.definitions.net/definition/presence.

[2] "Hypostasis." American Heritage® Dictionary of the English Language, Fifth Edition. Copyright © 2016 by Houghton Mifflin Harcourt Publishing Company. Accessed January 14, 2021. https://www.thefreedictionary.com/Hypostasis+(Christianity)

[3] Definition and synonyms of "plan" from the online English dictionary from MacMillan Education. Accessed January 14, 2021. https://www.macmillandictionary.com/us/dictionary/american/plan_2

[4] Easton, M. "Faith - Easton's Bible Dictionary." Blue Letter Bible. Last Modified June 19, 1996. Accessed January 14, 2021. https://www.blueletterbible.org/search/Dictionary/viewTopic.cfm?topic=ET00013022

[5] BibleGateway.com by Zondervan. "Women Issue Blood." Accessed January 14, 2021. https://www.biblegateway.com/resources/all-women-bible/Woman-Issue-Blood

[6] LearnersDictionary.com by Merriam-Webster. Definition of "complete." Accessed January 14, 2021. http://www.learnersdictionary.com/definition/complete

[7] Dictionary.com. Unabridged based on the Random House Unabridged Dictionary, © Random House Inc. Definition of "enlightened." Accessed January 14, 2021. https://www.dictionary.com/browse/enlighten

[8] Strong's Greek Lexicon (KJV). Blue Letter Bible. Accessed January 14, 2021. https://www.blueletterbible.org//lang/lexicon/lexicon.cfm?Strongs=g4102&t=KJV

[9] The American Heritage® Dictionary of Idioms by Christine Ammer. Definition of "good." Copyright © 2003, 1997 by The Christine Ammer 1992 Trust. Published by Houghton Mifflin Harcourt Publishing Company. All rights reserved. Accessed January 14, 2021. https://idioms.thefreedictionary.com/for+good

[10] Cambridge English Thesaurus © Cambridge University Press. Definition of "constantly." Accessed January 14, 2021. https://dictionary.cambridge.org/us/dictionary/english/constantly

[11] OxfordDictionaries.com. Definition of "praise." Accessed January 14, 2021. https://en.oxforddictionaries.com/definition/praise

[12] OxfordDictionaries.com. Definition of "devour." Accessed January 14, 2021. https://en.oxforddictionaries.com/definition/devour

[13] OxfordDictionaries.com. Definition of "assurance." Accessed January 14, 2021. https://en.oxforddictionaries.com/definition/assurance

[14] OxfordDictionaries.com. Definition of "unity." Accessed January 14, 2021. https://en.oxforddictionaries.com/definition/unity

[15] OxfordDictionaries.com. Definition of "known." Accessed January 14, 2021. https://en.oxforddictionaries.com/definition/known

[16] "Masterpiece." Merriam-Webster.com Dictionary, Merriam-Webster. Accessed January 14 2021. https://www.merriam-webster.com/dictionary/masterpiece.

[17] OxfordDictionaries.com. Definition of "child." Accessed January 14, 2021. https://en.oxforddictionaries.com/definition/child

[18] The Student Bible Dictionary, 2000, Holman Bible Publishers

[19] Dictionary.com. Unabridged based on the Random House Unabridged Dictionary, © Random House, Inc. 2021. Definition of "created." Accessed January 14, 2021. https://www.dictionary.com/browse/created

[20] OxfordDictionaries.com. Definition of "abundantly." Accessed January 14, 2021. https://en.oxforddictionaries.com/definition/abundantly

[21] Kadari, Tamar. "Hagar: Midrash and Aggadah." Jewish Women: A Comprehensive Historical Encyclopedia. 20 March 2009. Jewish Women's Archive. (Viewed on January 14, 2021) https://jwa.org/encyclopedia/article/hagar-midrash-and-aggadah.

[22] Dictionary.com. Unabridged based on the Random House Unabridged Dictionary, © Random House, Inc. 2021. Definition of "redeemed." Accessed January 14, 2021. https://www.dictionary.com/browse/redeemed

[23] Vine, W. "Restore - Vine's Expository Dictionary of New Testament Words." Blue Letter Bible. Last Modified June 24, 1996. Accessed January 14, 2021. https://www.blueletterbible.org/search/dictionary/viewTopic.cfm

[24] Thayer and Smith. Greek Lexicon entry for "Katartizo." The NAS New Testament Greek Lexicon, 1999. Accessed January 14, 2021. https://www.biblestudytools.com/lexicons/greek/nas/katartizo.html

[25] OxfordDictionaries.com. Definition of "patiently." Accessed January 14, 2021. https://en.oxforddictionaries.com/definition/patiently

[26] Dictionary.com. Unabridged based on the Random House Unabridged Dictionary, © Random House, Inc. 2021. Definition of "courage." Accessed January 14, 2021. https://www.dictionary.com/browse/courage

[27] Thayer and Smith. Greek Lexicon entry for "Katergazomai." The NAS New Testament Greek Lexicon, 1999. Accessed January 14, 2021. https://www.biblestudytools.com/lexicons/greek/nas/katergazomai.html

[28] "Accepted." Merriam-Webster.com Dictionary, Merriam-Webster. Accessed January 14, 2021. https://www.merriam-webster.com/dictionary/accepted. https://www.studylight.org/dictionaries/hbd/a/acceptance.html

[29] OxfordDictionaries.com. Definition of "submit." Accessed January 14, 2021. https://en.oxforddictionaries.com/definition/submit

[30] OxfordDictionaries.com. Definition of "truthful." Accessed January 14, 2021. https://en.oxforddictionaries.com/definition/truthful

[31] OxfordDictionaries.com. Definition of "bitter." Accessed January 14, 2021. https://en.oxforddictionaries.com/definition/bitter

[32] "Affliction." Merriam-Webster.com Dictionary, Merriam-Webster. Accessed January 14 2021. http://webstersdictionary1828.com/Dictionary/affliction

[33] "Renew." Merriam-Webster.com Dictionary, Merriam-Webster. Accessed January 14 2021. https://unabridged.merriam-webster.com/collegiate/renew

[34] "Discerning." Merriam-Webster.com Dictionary, Merriam-Webster. Accessed January 14 2021. https://www.merriam-webster.com/dictionary/discerning

[35] OxfordDictionaries.com. Definition of "grace." Accessed January 14, 2021. https://en.oxforddictionaries.com/definition/grace

[36] Definition of "reproach" from the Cambridge Academic Content Dictionary © Cambridge University Press) https://dictionary.cambridge.org/us/dictionary/english/reproach

[37] OxfordDictionaries.com. Definition of "integrity." Accessed January 14, 2021. https://en.oxforddictionaries.com/definition/integrity

[38] OxfordDictionaries.com. Definition of "heavenward." Accessed January 14, 2021. https://en.oxforddictionaries.com/definition/heavenward

[39] "Sanctify." Merriam-Webster.com Dictionary, Merriam-Webster. Accessed January 14 2021. https://www.merriam-webster.com/dictionary/sanctify

[40] Got Questions Ministries © Copyright 2002-2021. Definition of "sanctification. Accessed January 14, 2021. https://www.gotquestions.org/sanctification.html

[41] BibleGateway.com by Zondervan. "Maturity, Spiritual." Accessed January 14, 2021. https://www.biblegateway.com/resources/dictionary-of-bible-themes/5904-maturity-spiritual

[42] Lexico.com. Definition of "position." Accessed January 14, 2021. https://www.lexico.com/en/definition/position

[43] Smith, William, Dr. "Entry for 'Anointing,'" Smith's Bible Dictionary, 1901. Accessed January 14, 2021. https://www.biblestudytools.com/dictionary/anointing

[44] Stewart, D. "What Is the Gap Theory? (The Ruin and Reconstruction Theory?)." Blue Letter Bible. Last Modified 24 Apr, 2007. Accessed January 14, 2021. https://www.blueletterbible.org/faq/don_stewart/don_stewart_447.cfm

[45] "Divine," Clyx.com. Accessed January 14, 2021. https://clyx.com/term/divine.htm

[46] Cambridge English Thesaurus © Cambridge University Press. Definition of "revive." Accessed January 14, 2021. https://dictionary.cambridge.org/us/dictionary/english/revive

[47] The workbook *Coach Yourself with the Father* by Sally Hanan can be a great starting point for this. https://www.amazon.com/Coach-Yourself-Father-Pick-Your/dp/0991335082

[48] OxfordDictionaries.com. Definition of "comfort." Accessed January 14, 2021. https://en.oxforddictionaries.com/definition/comfort

[49] Definition of "season" from Webster's American Dictionary of the English Language, 1828. Accessed January 14, 2021. https://av1611.com/kjbp/kjv-dictionary/season.html

[50] Lexico.com. Definition of "work." Accessed January 14, 2021. https://www.lexico.com/en/definition/work

[51] "Thrive." Merriam-Webster.com Dictionary, Merriam-Webster. Accessed January 14 2021. https://www.merriam-webster.com/dictionary/thrive

About the Author

Jen Grice is a freelance writer for several Christian websites, a blogger, YouTuber, and a divorce coach. After publishing her first book, *You Can Survive Divorce*, in 2017, she knew God had many more books for her to write on the topic of Christian divorce and redemption.

When not writing or reading, Jen enjoys home organization, design, and décor, as well as fashion. She lives in Michigan though dreams of living on a tropical island, and is currently gearing herself up for her upcoming season of being an empty nester.

Resources

Purchase a Group Bible Study Leader's Guide at JenGrice.com/Shop

Look for the *Your Redemption Journey* companion workbook, coming later this year.

Stay up-to-date on new books and other divorce resources at JenGrice.com/resources, or sign up for emails from Jen at JenGrice.com/after-divorce-signup.

Let's be friends on social media (Jen actively responds as much as she can).

Facebook: fb.com/msjengriceauthor
Instagram: instagram.com/msjengrice
YouTube: youtube.com/c/jengrice
Twitter: twitter.com/msjengrice

More articles about rediscovering and having a stronger faith after divorce written by Jen:

https://jengrice.com/topic/faith

https://www.ibelieve.com/relationships/god-has-a-purpose-for-your-painful-divorce.html

https://www.ibelieve.com/slideshows/5-lies-every-divorced-woman-needs-to-stop-believing.html

Can You Help?

Reviews are everything to an author, because they mean a book is given more visibility. If you enjoyed this book, please review it on your favorite book review sites and tell your friends about it. Thank you!

Acknowledgments

Special thanks to my beta readers. You encouraged me and gave me your honest feedback about this book as I was still writing it.

Thanks to my Christian mentor, Sheila, for your words of wisdom that propelled me to learn and write more about these specific topics.

Lastly, thanks to my publishing team, my friends, and Sally at Inksnatcher and Jen at Line of Hope Creative Solutions—you understand my crazy, busy mind and translated that into a beautiful book, both inside and out. I could not have done all of this without you!

Made in the USA
Coppell, TX
12 October 2021

63903262R00177